WHITE PAPERS ON DISSENT

WHITE PAPERS ON DISSENT

Rethinking Art, Value, and Resistance Through Blockchain

Barbara Cueto

The MIT Press
Cambridge, Massachusetts
London, England

The MIT Press
Massachusetts Institute of Technology
77 Massachusetts Avenue
Cambridge, MA 02139
mitpress.mit.edu

The MIT Press would like to thank the anonymous peer reviewers who provided comments on drafts of this book. The generous work of academic experts is essential for establishing the authority and quality of our publications. We acknowledge with gratitude the contributions of these otherwise uncredited readers.

This book was set in ITC Stone Serif Std and Pangram by New Best-set Typesetters Ltd. Printed and bound in the United States of America.

Library of Congress Cataloging-in-Publication Data is available.

ISBN: 978-0-262-05669-4

10 9 8 7 6 5 4 3 2 1

EU Authorised Representative: Easy Access System Europe, Mustamäe tee 50, 10621 Tallinn, Estonia | Email: gpsr.requests@easproject.com

Para mis padres, por el pasado
Para Anton, para el futuro

CONTENTS

INTRODUCTION

I came to postcapitalist politics as many others do: in search of alternatives. Unsurprisingly, the path was winding. Growing up in Asturias, a small region in northern Spain, the future never seemed especially bright. The coastline is very close to mountain peaks, creating a dramatic landscape. Nature is harsh and beautiful. Rich in coal and zinc, Asturias industrialized rapidly, and for a time, mining and heavy industry thrived, and with them came strong workers' unions. But today, the region suffers: an aging population, the decline of coal mining, and an unsuccessful restructuring of heavy industries leave behind a lingering sense of stagnation.

Is there a way out of this spiral? In my search for possibilities, I encountered many books, art projects, and exhibitions about alternatives to the same extractivist capitalism that had rendered Asturias a lethargic region. The commons were featured almost as a dream of postcapitalism, a system that was neither purely private property nor simply controlled by the state, where a community collectively uses, maintains, and governs shared resources. Asturias, despite its industrial scars, is deeply rural. Agricultural commons continue to function and cooperative systems have built the country's largest dairy company. The alternative I was looking for had always been right in front of me. Maybe the way forward was to look backward. My research into commoning led me to confront issues of enclosure, extractivism, and sustainability. Yet, I questioned whether these older models could be updated. Could a better governance system make more resilient commons? Could we build systems that strengthen cooperativism and encourage collaboration across communities?

In 2016, I arrived in Seoul when massive demonstrations spread through the city demanding that the impeached president of South Korea be removed from office. Thousands of people holding lit candles in the middle of an incredibly cold winter seemed the fulfillment of a dream: members of civil society united, exercising their civil rights, created a political mass *with* agency. And they succeeded: the Constitutional Court upheld the impeachment by a vote of 8–0. Coming from Spain, where corruption often seems immune to public outrage, I had an epiphany. I arrived there with a fellowship to study new media art in South Korea, but this experience changed everything. I wanted to know more. I wanted to know how. I also traveled to Hong Kong in 2019 to see and experience the incredible and massive demonstrations against mainland China: another David versus Goliath fight. How could normal people armed only with an internet connection be a menacing force to a totalitarian state? We all know how this all ended, but the spirit and the energy in the city were unforgettable. These experiences opened up an unknown field to me, that of collective organizing using digital activism. I soon realized that the imprint of digital coordination had also influenced the subsequent artistic practices in the region. In another fellowship in Gwangju, my research culminated in an exhibition tracing the recent history of activism in South Korea and the effects on a practice that struck me as new: a mix of critique and activism heavily influenced by the affordances of different technologies—a sort of socially engaged tech-art assemblage.

Art, to me, has always been a way of thinking ahead, of sketching futures in the margins of the present. As a curator, I am drawn to artistic practices not only as spaces for reflection but also as laboratories of social life, where risk, refusal, and reinvention can unfold. Experimentation demands space in every sense: material, conceptual, and political. Technology has long offered fertile ground for this. The encounter between art and technology is not recent. In 1967, the nonprofit collective Experiments in Art and Technology (E.A.T.) brought together Bell Labs engineers with New York artists, choreographers, and composers. In this transdisciplinary organization, boundaries dissolved and new forms emerged. Technological experimentation was never a footnote to art history. It is part of its very texture: art responding to its moment by experimenting with the limits of what it can be. What drew me in in the first place was not just the invention of new tools, but also the emergence of new ways of thinking, perceiving, and relating. Art, especially in dialogue with technology, creates room for uncertainty, for questioning, for things not yet fully formed, and thus, still possible. It is the space for imagination. That openness is what attracted me. I have always seen artistic practice as a space where ideas can be tested in real time, where failure is not only allowed but also productive. Could this interplay between technology and art, therefore, become a ground for rethinking value, for prototyping other ways of living, and an incubator for systemic change?

In 2016, when I first traveled to South Korea, Web3 had begun to capture the imagination of artists, theorists, and political organizers. Many dismissed it as little more than speculative frenzy: meme coins, Ponzi schemes, financial excess. But I saw something else. I became enamored with this very complicated and clunky technology not so much because of its economics, but because of the ways it lets us imagine the world. Underlying the technology is a radical potential: a way to reimagine value, to build structures of collective governance, and to rethink cooperation beyond the state-market binary. And let's be honest—the future looks bleak. Political extremism, economic precarity, environmental collapse. The sense of systemic blockage has become overwhelming. Could this technology be the emancipatory tool I was looking for? Could it be the way of updating the commons-oriented economies and the sense of cooperation that I saw in my region? Could it embody the same desire for change that I encountered in Korea and Hong Kong?

And this is how and why I started this research.

This book proposes blockchain as social device to rehearse postcapitalist practices. A blockchain is a digital ledger used to track online transactions, and it is decentralized, meaning that its structure does not have a central point; all information is kept in nodes. This architecture allows for a wide range of applications, and in this book I explain how it can sustain alternative governance mechanisms, and the ways in which it can transform the notion of value. To say that the book is about politics is reductive. It is really about imagination, about the power of imagining the world otherwise. That is why I turned to the art world, to create propositions that embody this radical imagination, allowing us, the audience, to participate, to feel, to experience the dream of blockchain-driven postcapitalist politics. The relationship between technology and art is not one-sided: technology reshapes artistic practice, and art, in turn, reconfigures how we understand technology.

Someone might say that a particular technology cannot give all the answers. But maybe decentralized ledger technology can point out toward the right questions. I consider blockchain technology because of its radical approach to the future, desire for innovation, and ability to convey a utopia that is still underway, while representing today's yearning for change.

The intention of this book is not to suggest blockchain as the solution for every governance problem, monetary rearrangement, or imbalance in the power structure of the art world. Rather, it is dedicated to the exploration of blockchain as a tool for radical imagination. I focus not on specific outcomes, but on the vast range of possibilities that blockchain presents. The book delves into the ways blockchain makes us think, the structures it enables us to construct, and the paradigms it seeks to overthrow. Inevitably, it also considers the myriad threats blockchain technology will need to circumvent.

Blockchain is not a blank slate. It is more like a mirror, reflecting both the systems from which it emerges and the aspirations projected onto it. It has been embraced by venture capitalists and speculators, just as it has been reimagined by artists and activists seeking new forms of cooperation, care, and redistribution. Its architecture can be co-opted or contested, depending on how and by whom it is used. This ambiguity is not a flaw, but a condition that must be critically navigated. That is why it becomes crucial to approach blockchain politically before it can reconfigure social repercussions of hypercapitalism.

I do not consider blockchain as a whole to be the future savior of our unhealthy economy and the solution to our polarized governance. I am also not investigating only NFTs, or all artistic projects using blockchain. I am focusing my research on the artistic projects that "think" through the technology and are dedicated to social production and reproduction. I intend to formulate blockchain as a tool for radical imagination and a device that can reformulate a notion of value beyond market relations. For me, blockchain is a way to encapsulate desires and hopes of the social movements before us and, as a result, it also states dissent.

Instead of exploring the grand narratives of economic systems and their political and social connotations, I propose a careful meandering through the fringes of economic discourse and the outskirts of the art world. To do so, I concentrate on looking for alternative vocabularies and artistic proposals to create a weak theory. The inspiration for this approach comes from queer theory scholar Eve Sedgwick, whose concept of weak theory does not focus on all-encompassing, already existing theoretical frameworks, but limits its reach and localizes its purview.[1] The intention is not to create a theory to explain all symptoms, but to look for the deviant, the opening, the alternative, or the divergent and dissenting discourses. If hard theory has enforced the hegemonic systems of thinking and acting, in contrast, weak theory can de-exoticize power and investigate more pedestrian forms, whereby a differentiated landscape of force, constraint, energy, and freedom can open up.[2] Also influenced by this notion, J. K. Gibson-Graham aimed at liberating languages from discursive subordination.[3] (J. K. Gibson-Graham is the name shared by feminist economic geographers Julie Graham and Katherine Gibson.) And these economic geographers have been a great inspiration for this book and the curatorial projects that gave rise to it.

My curatorial practice has been an immense resource for this book, allowing me to invite artists, technologists, and scholars to this act of collective radical imagination. I have curated talks, workshops, performances, and LARPs, and conducted plenty of interviews to learn from the actors that were shaping my thinking and to show others this world of possibilities. The projects at Asian Cultural Centre (ACC) in Gwangju; Van Abbemuseum in Eindhoven, the Netherlands; and Singapore Art Museum are the thread that stitches together the fabric of this book. Sometimes I mention these projects specifically, but many others are present as glimpses of conversations and moments of togetherness. But three interviews I've done are presented in their entirety: with feminist economist Katherine

Gibson (from the collective J. K. Gibson-Graham), media theorist Geert Lovink, and art historian and artist Gregory Sholette. They were fundamental pieces in my research, and turning points in my argumentation. They represent the three interlocking threads that built this book: economic thinking, activism, and art history. Excerpts of these three interviews are inserted throughout the text as moments of reflection and provocation. One can read these snippets then jump back into the normal flow of the book; they function both as afterthoughts and inspirations to sharpen our way of thinking and illuminate our understanding of the issues at stake.

I see this book as a repertoire rather than an archive because of the way the curatorial projects have shaped it. Participating in and researching them created embodied knowledges instead of theory-like awareness. That is why I refer to the practice of blockchain rather than the theory that produces it. A repertoire, unlike an archive, expands the meaning of knowledge itself because it includes "all those acts usually thought of as ephemeral, non-reproducible knowledge," as performance scholar Diana Taylor explains.[4] And this is why I look into the artists working with blockchains, because their projects are rehearsals of postcapitalist worlds. Their projects unfold not as fixed statements, but as open-ended invitations, where audiences become coauthors of meaning, fellow travelers in the collective act of inventing a world post-crisis. The embodied knowledges I refer to here are able to enact, continue, and transmit the feelings of practicing the technology, keeping the learning alive through its repetition. In the book, I mention artist-led blockchain projects at different stages: proof-of-work, prototypes, ideas, or white papers working dApps (decentralized applications). I do not differentiate between them because I talk about potentialities, about rethinking and reinventing the technology to fulfill the dreams that go way beyond the financial aspects.

In spite of all the trustlessness or disintermediation, decentralized ledger technology like any other technology is a tool created *with* and *for* people. That is why I am talking about embodied knowledge here, rather than hard theory. Three entwined concepts come to represent those embodiments: structures of belonging, dislocated time, and infrastructure of critique. They symbolize what blockchain achieves, not what it is designed and programmed to do. The first concept, structures of belonging, conveys a kin architecture where the participants/users/constituents of a project are united by a shared social imaginary. This affective connection is enacted prefiguratively, as distributed ledger technology operates in a different temporal matrix—I called this feeling of time, the second concept, dislocated time. The third concept, infrastructure of critique, alludes to how the technology scaffolds an implicit critique to the very system that it upholds. To explain these three concepts, I refer to different artist-driven blockchain projects that reveal the texture of feeling created by cold, synthetic technology. They are neither demonstrations or assemblies, nor socially engaged projects or institutional critique nested in the museums. They are somewhere in between, and that interconnection is what endows them with political agency. They are theory-in-the-making as well as collective experiences that—once enacted—allow us to see the world *otherwise*.

Within this book, I position blockchain not only as a technical infrastructure, but also as a site of contestation, a tool for rethinking the systems we take for granted. This raises difficult, necessary questions: How do we govern ourselves collectively? Can we redefine value beyond markets? What role does technology play in shaping political possibility? Could art hold the political agency to actively shape these emerging structures? I do not offer definitive answers, nor do I seek to. Instead, I explore the tensions, contradictions, and openings that emerge when art and technology intersect with postcapitalist thought. It is not about predicting the future. It is about making space for it to emerge.

OVERVIEW

The book provides an analysis through two complementary angles: the politics within the technology and its aesthetic experimentations. On the one hand, I explore how the different uses of blockchain technology can support new socio-technological imaginaries based on community and commons-oriented economies. On the other hand, I explore how artists working with blockchains give rise to new forms of aesthetic resistance that recreate, in the present, a desired unwritten future. They turn thus into pre-enactments of a multiverse of agonistic proposals that challenge our perception of value. Because of their distinct use of the technology and their different approach to art making, I grouped these projects together under the name Critical Blockchain Art. In three numbered chapters, the book unpacks these concepts explaining the technology beyond blockchains' technical characteristics, rooting its artistic practices within the lineage of institutional critique and socially engaged art. This perspective requires deep-seated reflection on technological potential in times of crisis, and the role of art in overcoming crisis.

The book traces the political potential of blockchain beyond its technical design and market-driven narratives. After outlining the characteristics of its affordances, I examine how distributed ledger technologies support forms of social production that operate outside market logics, structured instead around community-defined, non-capitalocentric values. Chapter 1 invites readers to unlearn conventional ideas about value and to consider how blockchain could be repurposed as a site for collective autonomy and place-based politics. I explore how artists and activists appropriate blockchain to prototype new forms of cooperation and dissent, building on the aspirations and unfinished projects of the social movements of the 2010s. Their practices reveal how this technology, often seen as abstract or opaque, becomes a material and political device for rehearsing new social and political imaginaries. In doing so, blockchain emerges not simply as technical infrastructure, but also as a contested cultural space where new sociopolitical possibilities are tested and negotiated.

In chapter 2, I introduce and frame Critical Blockchain Art, situating this emerging practice within a broader art historical lineage. Moving beyond questions of medium specificity, I understand digital art as a form of critique responsive to the conditions of a postdigital society. Its roots extend to the avant-garde's spirit of rupture and its utopian longings; to the analytical rigor of institutional critique; to the commitment of socially engaged practices; and to the peer-to-peer (P2P) infrastructures of digital activism. Through these genealogies, I examine how artists experimenting with technology generate new forms of interaction that challenge established models of display, mediation, and reproduction, while encouraging expanded modes of spectatorship, collaboration, and co-creation. Against this backdrop, chapter 2 of the book traces the emergence of artistic practices engaging blockchains, establishing a distinct lineage that both inherits these traditions and sets them apart, toward new directions.

Building on the previous chapters, chapter 3 explores the political agency of Critical Blockchain Art, focusing on how its practices enact dissent and prefigure alternative futures. Here I introduce three interrelated concepts—structures of belonging, dislocated time, and infrastructure of critique—to describe the social and affective dimensions of these projects. Together, the projects capture how blockchain-mediated initiatives cultivate shared imaginaries, operate beyond linear political timeframes, and embed critique within technical infrastructures themselves. Far from offering technological solutions, these projects use blockchain as a space to test and rehearse new forms of cooperation and collective life. In this sense, blockchain operates as both a tool for imagination and a structure that organizes dissent, turning critique into form. By working with the plasticity of its affordances, artists prototype surrogate worldviews and renegotiate entrenched financial, political, and social orders. The political agency of Critical Blockchain Art lies in this capacity: to envision and materialize counter-hegemonic imaginaries, embedding them within infrastructures that not only resist the present but also rehearse the possibility of other futures.

White Papers on Dissent departs from the familiar economic framings of blockchain to position it instead as a social apparatus capable of reformulating value beyond the market. This shift grounds my focus on those projects I call Critical Blockchain Art. Emerging at the intersection of artistic and technological experimentation, and political imagination, this practice envisions alternative social worlds in response to the crises of neoliberalism. Critical Blockchain Art inherits not only a desire for transformation, but also the drive to forge new forms of aesthetic resistance that embed critique into infrastructure, cultivate belonging, and prefigure the contours of worlds otherwise.

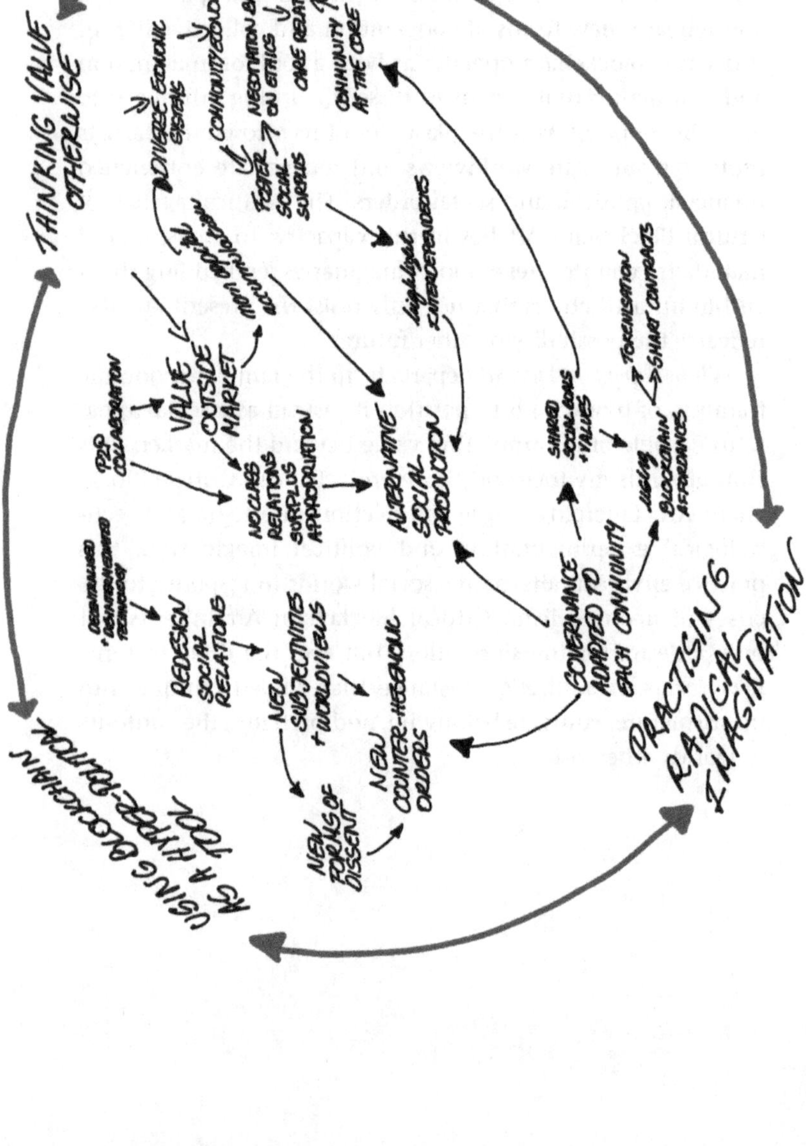
THINKING VALUE OTHERWISE
USING BLOCKCHAIN AS A HYPER-POLITICAL TOOL
PRACTISING RADICAL IMAGINATION
DECENTRALISED + DISINTERMEDIATED TECHNOLOGY
REDESIGN SOCIAL RELATIONS
NEW SUBJECTIVITIES + WORLDVIEWS
NEW FORMS OF DISSENT
NEW COUNTER-HEGEMONIC ORDERS
P2P COLLABORATION
NO CLASS RELATIONS SURPLUS APPROPRIATION
VALUE OUTSIDE MARKET
DIVERSE ECONOMIC SYSTEMS
COMMUNITY ECONOMIES
FOSTER SOCIAL SURPLUS
NEGOTIATION BASED ON ETHICS
CARE RELATIONS
COMMUNITY AT THE CORE
highlight INTERDEPENDENCIES
ALTERNATIVE SOCIAL PRODUCTION
GOVERNANCE ADAPTED TO EACH COMMUNITY
SHARED SOCIAL GOALS + VALUES
USING BLOCKCHAIN AFFORDANCES
TOKENISATION
SMART CONTRACTS

FIGURE 0.1

1 POLITICS OF BLOCKCHAIN

In France, when the new labor law was released in 2016, a journalist noted that there was a clash of two minorities: a governmental minority and a minority of demonstrators in front of a population of spectators. Between 2015 and 2019, Spain held four presidential elections. In the United States, the 2020 Democratic primaries started with twenty-nine candidates. Brexit lasted three years and launched four prime ministers in rapid succession: Brexit aftershocks jettisoned Boris Johnson, who was followed by seven weeks of Liz Truss, then two years of Rishi Sunak, and after him Keir Starmer. During the same timeframe, Apple reported a record revenue of 394.33 billion USD in 2022[1] and Amazon's annual revenue peaked in 2024 with 637.959 billion USD.[2] In the same period, social media apps ranked among the most downloaded features on phones across the world, gaining unprecedented influence. The conglomerate Meta owns three of the fifteen most globally downloaded apps of all time, and at the top of this list sits TikTok.[3] As the population is endemically questioning the traditional functions of the Westphalian nation-state, such as sovereignty and authority,[4] it also consents, almost without reservation, to be reunited under the empire of the cloud.

The start of the 2010s decade is tinted with political fragmentation on one side, and an overwhelming concentration of power in digital corporations on the other. "What makes our situation so ominous, is the all-pervasive sense of blockage. There is no clear way out, and the ruling elite is clearly losing its ability to rule," reasons philosopher Slavoj Žižek.[5] Political distrust inadvertently prompted the conditions that the monoliths of Silicon Valley used to construct their own power infrastructure. Their algorithmic power not only transforms the manner in which we access information, but also molds the form of our socio-technical systems.[6] As the Invisible Committee collective asserts, "The great builders of infrastructure have the means for which the fascists only have the folkloric discourse."[7] This new(er) regime of control has surpassed Lenin's notion of the state as an apparatus of coercion,[8] because these digital transnational corporations exert a type of oppression that is ubiquitous and exhaustive: it defines the way we access the world and relate to each other. That's why this book starts by pondering the interrelationship of politics and technology as a way to insist on the need to forge political digital spaces.

Today's situation is reminiscent of Plato's cave allegory, but here the end user has become addicted and manipulated, constantly tweeting, posting, and checking their smart devices in a sort of neurosis à la Frantz Fanon. Far from activating political consciousness, we all languish, unable to trigger a political reform that overpowers political fragmentation. As private and public actors become ever more encroached, so does surveillance and, with it, algorithmic power pervasively grows, affecting all mechanisms of communication. As early as 1948, legal philosopher Zechariah Chafee[9] explained that the media was pivotal in forming political and cultural consciousness, and their role in influencing democratic processes is undisputed. Fast-forward sixty years and here we are: fake news rampantly running across the internet, and parliaments around the world at the highest levels of polarization. As we all know, these problems are far from being solved, and they are often enhanced with a sense of ecological and economic crisis looming ahead. The future looks bleak.

Media theorist Geert Lovink speaks of the "stack of crises" that defines our contemporary condition. But what can we do in the face of such a pervasive sense of collapse? Or perhaps more urgently: how can we even begin to imagine another future when this crisis of feeling clouds every step forward? This book begins by responding to that question through a speculative gesture: a collective act of imagination. In chapter 1, I propose we think *as if* we had already overcome today's struggles. This "as-if" becomes a necessary method, not of denial, but of imaginative resistance. It is a way to reclaim our capacity to envision futures beyond exhaustion, beyond extraction. Artists, I argue, are central to this process. By engaging critically with technologies like blockchain, they offer novel ways of thinking about social, political, and economic change. Artists do not merely react to technology; they challenge its assumptions, reframe its uses, and propose alternative ways of being. This book focuses on the work of artists who engage with blockchain not for speculative financial gain but to experiment with new forms of social organization, solidarity, and value production. Their work opens up possibilities for rethinking how we might use technology to build more inclusive, democratic, and equitable systems.

To ground these ideas, I will begin by explaining the workings behind blockchain so I then can address the potential of using blockchains for political redesign. What values (currently unrecognized or devalued in our hypercapitalist systems) might serve as the pillars of future social and political institutions? This question opens an inquiry into the emancipatory potential of blockchain technology, which acts as breeding ground to understand the ways in which artists radically imagine its potential. But instead of focusing on the financial discussion that populate the ecosystem, I steer the discussion toward less discussed social and political aspects.

I explore how distributed ledger technologies might enable forms of social production that operate outside the market, structured instead around community-defined, non-capitalocentric values. Chapter 1 is thus a call to unlearn the market-centric conception of value and to begin imagining how blockchain could embody alternative systems of worth that artists based on their experiment of postcapitalist practices. Ultimately, I propose reframing blockchain as a site of place-based politics: a cultural and technological apparatus capable of sustaining new forms of collective autonomy. In this vision, artists are not just participants in the blockchain ecosystem; they are key agents of change, driving forward innovative uses of blockchain that challenge and transform its dominant narratives. Through their practices, they invite us to rethink what is possible, and how new forms of collective action might emerge. In this way, I suggest that blockchains can be harnessed as infrastructures for new sociopolitical imaginaries, rooted in the dissident energies of the social movements of the 2010s and aligned with the plural values of a world still in the making. This is the rich substrate used by artists across the world to rethink the potential of different social lives anchored on a blockchain structure.

ALGORITHMIC TRUST IN TIMES OF CRISIS

Blockchain is, literally, a public chain of sequential chunks of information irreversibly linked one after the other and cryptographically encrypted, which produces an immutable ledger of transactions shared by all network nodes. The result is a tamper-proof "public record repository for documents, contracts, properties, and assets . . . which can be used to embed information and instructions, with a wide range of applications," as Marcella Atzori, blockchain scholar, clarifies.[10] Accordingly, this decentralized technology has the ability to facilitate an automated code-based transnational system that offers an alternative financial and contractual tool to organize social activity.[11] The technology is a permanent, distributed digital ledger.

Although this decentralized technology is often associated with financialization, its possibilities are manifold, since it provides mechanisms both for coordination and rule enforcement.[12] As a result, it enables new forms of governance that are native to the affordances of the underlying technology, which include disintermediation and alternative frameworks beyond central authorities.[13] That is the reason why it is considered a legal technology that can spark institutional innovation.[14]

The radical potential of blockchain relies on the rigid temporal matrix in which it operates. All past transactions in a blockchain are immutable because they are cryptographically recorded; furthermore, the future is programable through smart contracts, which are something like a miniprogram that executes an agreement once predefined conditions are met. Instead of relying on a person, institution, or intermediary to enforce a contract, the rules are written in software and carried out by the network itself. This is all thanks to the main feature of blockchain: trustlessness.

The year 2008 marks a before and after in our economic systems: Lehman Brothers filed for bankruptcy on September 15; some will remember the white paper "Bitcoin: A Peer-to-Peer Electronic Cash," released under the pseudonym Satoshi Nakamoto. These events occurred only two month apart.[15] And what we all certainly remember is what happened after the Great Recession: a string of social movements that display the great divide between politics and society. We are still feeling the aftershocks of that white paper. Satoshi Nakamoto proposed a mysterious "trustless" digital currency at the point when the trustworthiness of central governments was in question (a state from which Europe has not yet recovered).[16] Trust, as a social adhesive, is an intrinsically human notion, yet Nakamoto managed to reroute it through blockchain, generating a synthetic version that has the potential to articulate new forms of resistance. Therefore, chapter 1 considers how trust can be manufactured and the sociopolitical implications of this.

Blockchain offers a method to algorithmically generate trust and, in turn, we collectively decide to endow its tokens with value, as we do with any other currency, be it a meme coin or a euro. The first blockchain's tokens were the famous Bitcoins, whose value has cycled between periods of sharp price increases ("bull markets") and significant declines ("bear markets"), in many cases coinciding with political events such as military conflicts (e.g., the Ukraine war), or the imposition of martial law in South Korea. Bitcoin's instability has raised concerns among regulators worldwide, as well as citizens worried about the great ecological toll caused by the high processing power needed to produce a token. The technical characteristics of blockchain trustlessness are multilayered. "People are represented through arbitrary digital keys, which eliminate the contextual factor that humans use to evaluate trust-worthiness," explains legal scholar Kevin Werbach.[17] On top of that, transactions are cryptographic proofs that are verifiable mathematically, and every single full node has a complete and accurate copy of all transactions on the blockchain. Consequently, there are no administrative nodes or hierarchical relationships and, correspondingly, neither censorship nor interference is possible.[18]

Bitcoin was one of the first technologies able to solve the thought experiment from computer science called the Byzantine Generals Problem.[19] This means that it overcame the potential lack of reliability in a transaction and encompassed for the first time a method to solve it, called the Byzantine Fault Tolerance (BFT) algorithm. As a result, all parties involved can find consensus and trust the ledger, even if some of the information might be inaccurate. Nakamoto's solution is called proof-of-work, a consensus mechanism that validates the transactions on the Bitcoin's blockchain and updates the nonmodifiable public database. To do so, a process called mining solves a difficult and time-consuming mathematical puzzle, called a hash, which is how a block is validated with a unique signature.[20] The reward for validating the next transaction (and therefore adding a block to the chain) is a token, which is a Bitcoin. The chance to win is related to the mining speed, and that is proportional to the computing power spent. As the competition increases among miners due to the scarcity of Bitcoin, its environmental toll rises too, because miners need enormous amounts of energy to process the puzzle.[21]

But a lot has changed since 2008, and consensus mechanisms are not just proof-of-work. There are many other possibilities that are more cost-efficient, such as proof-of-stake (POS). Instead of mining and its consequent use of processing power, POS is "based on game-theoretic incentives to promote compliant behaviour."[22] In this way, a node validates blockchain transactions proportionally to the amount of the ownership stake. In other words, it can validate as many coins as it holds: if it has 6 percent of the digital currency, it can therefore "mine" 6 percent of the total coins. After years in the making, Ethereum migrated to POS in September 2022, reducing their energy consumption by 99.95 percent.

Back to trustlessness. All blockchain infrastructures are able to manufacture trust effectively, because the algorithm creates a type of consensus that is unrelated to the trustworthiness of the agents or the message. Only the final ledger is reliable because of algorithmic validation, and its cycle of value creation and value acquisition. Reciprocally, the network of peers (miners) agrees that the token is a valuable reward that is worth the resolution of the mathematical puzzle. In contrast, P2P coordination is sustained by traditional trust, based on relationships, flexibility to adjust to solve problems, and a shared ethical perspective on how to deal with the commons while supporting the community.[23] However, blockchain trustlessness presents productive advantages for a P2P community, specifically because voluntary participation in the system is sustained through a distributed architecture where decision-making processes are coded on a protocol that is open source, immutable, and neutral. All the data is owned by all the nodes, and all the transactions are auditable. In this way, "it [distributed architecture] can overcome frictions and failures inherent in [the] decision-making process of centralised organisations (e.g. lack of transparency, corruption, coercion, etc.)."[24] This will come in handy later in my argumentation, because blockchains offers a resilient structure to support a translocal commons-oriented community.

Bitcoin offers an alternative to fiat money in times of crisis, but Ethereum, another blockchain-based structure, created a whole autonomous universe of tools with a much more nuanced form of agency and cooperation, which translated into an even greater capacity for self-organization. Ethereum is a cryptocurrency platform that is a Turing-complete virtual machine and programming language that can create and publish distributed applications.[25] Ethereum's most radical feature is the smart contract: a self-enforcing agreement embedded in computer code managed by a blockchain. In this way, smart contracts provide mechanisms for efficiently managing tokenized assets and access rights between two or more parties.[26] Essentially, smart contracts are autonomous, inasmuch as once they are running, they need no further communication. And this means that they will be forever and ever replicating themselves, without any external influence. They can be self-sufficient, which means they can raise funds by providing services or issuing equity, and also spend funds on storage or processing power, if needed. Lastly, they are distributed and self-executing across all the nodes of the network.[27]

Another fundamental innovation in Ethereum is decentralized autonomous organizations (DAOs). "As self-executing software running on a distributed blockchain, a DAO doesn't need any owners in the traditional sense. It simply operates and interacts with the world accordingly to its code."[28] Constructed using smart contracts, the DAO is able to perform tasks as if it were a corporation, but it can do so without the influence of any central government and is only controlled by shareholders.[29] A DAO implies that a form of organization holds a governance system, which provides decision-making capacities based on the pre-specified or preapproved tasks in relation to certain events or changing conditions. Rain, a drop in a stock price, or political upheaval can count as determining factors to alter the outcome of a task. That's why Oracles exist. Oracles can be human or things like APIs (application programming interfaces) and other external data feeds. They collect external input that is algorithmically processed and, with it, the DAO independently makes a decision. The participants only have indirect influence since they can provide input but cannot control its behavior.[30] A DAO can thus replicate the effects, functions, and operations of a physical-world business model, yet can avoid the costs related to its local jurisdiction, such as licensing, registration, insurance, or taxes.[31] Furthermore, a DAO can sustain itself autonomously. This means that it can effectively behave like a corporation, collecting funds or distributing internal capital (in the form of tokens) to reward investors or participants (as in workers) for their contributions.[32] In addition, a DAO can expand over time to supply services or labor "in exchange for digital tokens that provide the token holder with specific privileges."[33] The owner of the tokens can, thus, use them to acquire goods or services provided by the DAO, or in the case of profits, to be accordingly compensated. And this is at the core of the desire of many creatives using blockchains: to overcome the pitfalls of previous systems by creating new DAO-shaped institutions that act translocally, and independently from the powers of the market.

In summary, blockchain is a radical technological innovation that can promote alternative socio-economic structures, thanks to the provision of automated and trustless transactions. This is how artists work with it: as an agent of change that can be used to redesign its relations to finance, government, and society at large, and implicitly readdress power relations.[34] Owing to its decentralized and disintermediated governance system, blockchain overcomes centralized coercion and provides a system with horizontal hierarchies and distributed coordination mechanisms that endow individuals with higher stakes in terms of agency and self-determination. Hence, blockchain is able to coordinate epistemic crowds that can embed their values and social goals into the code.[35] As a result, it can create an independent system of governance providing algorithmic resistance.

However, while blockchain has the capacity to support decentralized and collectivized forms of governance, it remains embedded in the broader logic of capitalist development. Its environmental impact, speculative use, and uneven accessibility all point to its limitations as a truly emancipatory infrastructure. These contradictions must be taken seriously if we are to assess its political relevance. Rather than presenting blockchain as inherently radical, I argue that its radical potential emerges from how it is activated: by whom, for what purpose, and within what context. The technology is not neutral, but its affordances can be used to question hegemonic structures and experiment with alternatives. This book is concerned with those artistic practices that mobilize blockchain toward that end, not as a cure, but as a prompt for rethinking how we organize, value, and relate to each other.

Artists play a crucial role as early adopters and critical practitioners. They not only challenge the commercial and financial narratives that dominate blockchain discourse but also shape the conversation around its social, ethical, and political implications. Artists bring forward imaginative and speculative uses of technology, extending its capabilities into realms that transcend economic models and, in doing so, create spaces where alternative values can be explored. In the context of blockchain, artists are important because they can reframe the technology's role in society by asking vital questions about power, autonomy, and collective governance. By engaging with blockchain critically, they provide models for a more inclusive and equitable future, one that reimagines existing systems rather than simply replicating them.

Artists working with blockchains perceive the technology not as a mere financial tool set, but as an apparatus that can be deployed for producing pockets of resistance in the everyday. But before we consider the political potential of blockchain and artists' practices, I need to go back to the very essence of the political game: value systems.

QUEERING ECONOMIC LANGUAGES

Although this might seem simplistic, we all know that there are many types of values. We usually use the plural sense, as anthropologist David Graeber remarks, to encompass, for example, the aesthetic value of art, ecological values, or family and religious values.[36] However, if we don't have a universal measuring tape with one single system of value, we are left with multiple sets of heterogeneous, unrelated values. This translates into the current interpretation of an implicit hierarchy. Capitalist values are higher because they are countable, whereas noncapitalist values are lower in the ranking since they are incalculable. This process is discursive and, therefore, it also holds a potential: we can also choose to reconfigure the economy alternatively.

But how do we define value? Value is a very complex notion that we usually associate with money. To think about value otherwise is an act of reckoning, as we acknowledge the extent of its entanglement with capitalist thought. Value is expressed as a factor of exchange and, generally, its status is represented by money. Our perception of commodity exchange is a complex puzzle, whereby property sits at the core of capitalist thought, and with it, concepts like scarcity, natural order, command of possession, and labor as the source of wealth accumulation.[37]

Despite this complexity, the idea of value often starts with a basic assertion: value equals money. When people engage in a financial transaction, the goal, Marx observes, is money.[38] It is the ultimate embodiment of value. To complete that equation, the value of commodities is related to the amount of human labor that it took to produce them.[39] Therefore, value equals money that equals labor. Ricardo specifies that value can be calculated proportionally to the "man-hours" invested in the making.[40] Employers do not buy worker hours for a specific job or task; rather, they buy the *capacity* for work to be done during a particular period of time. This raises a question: When labor cannot be accounted for in purchasable hours of work, how is its correlative value proportionally measured? This leads in turn to another question: What could be considered valuable if we move away from these market-related concepts?

The theory of value is one of the classic, most repeated, better-researched fundaments of economic thought. That is no coincidence. This theory explains the price of goods and services, which we all have to deal with whether we like it or not. Theory of value ranges from why goods and services are priced as they are, to how to calculate their correct price, as well as how value comes about. If we want to understand blockchain as a social apparatus, I need to explain how a technology relates to the labor theory of value and to the exchange value theory. In the first case, labor theory of value connects to, obviously, labor, meaning that the value of a good is proportional to the amount of necessary labor that took to produce it. And that is why, as Marx would say, the working class is exploited by capitalism, because of the dissociation between price and value. In the second case, exchange value theory addresses how to exchange the value of a commodity for another. And this is the mother of all problems—because how can we compare values in our capitalist society if we don't have the market as intermediary?

Reconsidering value beyond capital relations is a complex matter with many possible answers. My argumentation is grounded on the work of the collective J. K. Gibson-Graham on diverse economic systems (as noted earlier, economic geographers Katherine Gibson and Julie Graham share this author name).[41] Although they don't specifically mention value, I try to continue their reasoning to reframe this notion as diverse, fluid, socially aware, and socially responsive.

Barbara Cueto: Your work on community economies has been very influential in my research, especially the idea and role of language. I take blockchain as another code language and as a rhetorical device that can enact language politics. Could you start by explaining this relationship between language, agency, and the economy?

Katherine Gibson: Our interest (with the late Julie Graham) was in saying, what is it that is stopping us from theorizing and enacting a postcapitalist world? One of the reasons we identified was this kind of language that was centered

> on what we call capitalocentrism. If we were trying to move beyond, we felt it's necessary to create a different kind of language of economy in which there is value given to, or emphasis and agency given to economic diversity that could be seen as operating, not only in the kind of a subordinated relationship to capitalist accumulation, but could have its own dynamics and its own trajectories and agency and so on. The language of a diverse economy was very important to us in terms of trying to deconstruct that capitalocentrism. And I guess language is important because if we don't have a way of talking about something, it's very hard to imagine and enact something else.

Language, as Judith Butler argues, has the power to create the effects that it names.[42] This means that language does not simply describe reality but also actively brings it into being. Words have performative power. In her work, Butler explains that gender is not an essence but a repeated performance sustained by normative language and social acts. By destabilizing and queering those linguistic categories, Butler shows that alternative modes of existence can flourish. If we want to perform values that move beyond the entrenched oppositions of capitalist versus noncapitalist, we must equally queer our economic languages. Just as the undoing of binary gender categories opened the horizon for other forms of embodiment and recognition, so too must we develop vocabularies that resist being trapped in familiar economic logics of scarcity, accumulation, or profit. Artists, as I will argue in chapter 2, have long carried this endeavor forward. They question, twist, and reinvent the languages that organize social life, including those based on binary systems. With blockchains, this mission continues in a new way: artistic practices experiment with vocabularies that reimagine and queer economies that gesture toward new postcapitalist futures.

The new and rich economic languages proposed by J. K. Gibson-Graham destabilize and dislocate the seemly identification between the economy and the rules of capitalism, which prompts counterhegemonic discursive projects of subversion. These new counter-hegemonic languages of a diverse economy can be put to work in very different scenarios, which result in diverse formulations of value that share a social dimension. Through them, it is possible to explore the multidimensional nature of economic existence. This shift implies overcoming class politics, and, thus, this language abandons the limiting and limited subject positions of consumer, worker, self-employed, unemployed, capitalist entrepreneur, and investor. Identity is, as a consequence, considered beyond the surplus appropriation structures of Louis Althusser,[43] and moves away from the struggles of capitalism, as per the regimens of value of Arjun Appadurai.[44]

Subverting capitalist dominance over the language of value calls for a new lexicon of economic diversity that could perform different economies. J. K. Gibson-Graham propose that we "re-politicise the economy by challenging the representation of capitals as the necessarily and naturally dominant form (or identity) of economy."[45] To reframe value beyond the market thus indicates a shift from the distinctive capitalocentric social imaginary composed by individual wealth, freedom, calculative rationality, competitive individualism, unburdened consumption, and well-being trickled down to all.[46] If we queer economic languages, we world-build an alternative. This act of world-building is not only conceptual but also imaginative and embodied. It signals the emergence of distinct social imaginaries, ones that loosen the grip of capitalocentric thinking and allow for other modes of relation, exchange, and value. Artists are especially attuned to this process. Their capacity to perform, simulate, and inhabit these alternatives invites us to experience futures not yet realized but already felt. This is the generative role of artistic practices within the blockchain space and the reason I have been drawn to them throughout this work.

This change in the capitalist imaginary alters the understanding of value and opens up a multiform and plural conceptualization of value derived from the three axes of diverse economic systems: different types of labor, commensurability, and surplus negotiation. Gibson-Graham insist that we "approach economic relationships as something to be contingently rather than deterministically configured,"[47] and that economic value then becomes free from the traditional rules of governing the economy and liberated from its mechanical logics. The exercise of liberation from a capitalocentric vernacular becomes a performative act. Devoid of these connotations, a new noncapitalist existence arises. This state of becoming is engendered, as Butler maintains, because power is assumed by the subject, and the same acceptance is what becomes the instrument for that subject's becoming.[48] This process of being and becoming is always active. Power is in continuous repetition, ritualized in practices that need to be broken. This is, intrinsically, the intention of Gibson-Graham, who state that "our objective has been to dis-order the capitalist economic langue, to queer it and thereby dislocate capitalocentrism's hegemony. In this space thus produced, we see opportunities for new economic becomings—sites where ethical decisions can be made, power can be negotiated and transformations forged."[49]

These diverse economic existences thus are not influenced by capitalocentric values. Those values are only produced in factories and only create commodities destined to be exchanged in a commensurable manner, as Marx would say.[50] In contrast, values that are produced outside the workplace are meant to circulate instead of being traded, because they are related to social production instead.[51] Precisely, those nonmarket transactions are at the core of these community economies, and the commensurability is socially negotiated, highlighting the interdependencies among all subjects in economic decision-making.[52] This means that in community economies the labor theory of value becomes obsolete. There is no surplus appropriation because there is no cycles-sequestering surplus, as there is no dissociation between price and value. One could think of barter, cooperatives, time banks, or mutual aid systems. In them, as I mentioned before, class politics disintegrate, because categories like worker, consumer, or self-employed are rendered ineffective. Organizing their negotiations are four ethical coordinates: necessity, surplus, consumption, and commons.[53] Community economies implicate a process of "recognising and revaluing a broader network of care-relationships that are central to all ecologies and economies."[54] As an analogy to diverse economic systems, I call these "diverse values," and they entail a counter-hegemonic discursive process that underlines the social aspects in the idea of value.

Barbara Cueto: I wonder about the "quality" of value. If we end up measuring with capitalocentric tools, wouldn't this implicitly mean to take away something out of the process of commoning that relates to community and care? For example, if you quantify care, wouldn't [that] also mean losing a little bit of this texture of feeling that goes within it? And, then, wouldn't we be just making marketable things that fortunately have escaped from the cycle of capitalism?

Katherine Gibson: I think that's an empirical question. I don't think it can be answered in an abstract way. I think you have to put it into a social context in order to see if that is undermining the nature of the care or not. Asking those kind of endpoint questions is kind of a philosophical exercise. I think it is useful to look at something in context: what would blockchain need to look like in order to make the care richer, for instance. And that is to me a really interesting, a practical and theoretical kind of question.

The language of community economy reconfigures value by making visible those interdependencies. One cannot undertake the endeavor of radically imagining the notion of value without asserting the obvious: our perception is influenced by Western thought. Non-Western perspectives in anthropology and ethnography provide an insightful framework that help one to understand value differently, and these theories of value procure a much more nuanced and useful knowledge for the task of this book, that of radically imagining blockchain.

The work of anthropologist Marilyn Strathern has greatly influenced my thought in this regard. Her work focused on Melpa-speaking inhabitants of the Mount Hagen area in Papua New Guinea, like Marcel Mauss's "The Gift" or *Gifts and Commodities* by Christopher Gregory, where she also investigates the gift economies. Strathern contrasts Melanesian gift economies with Euro-American commodity logic. She explores how value is created and circulated differently in these systems, challenging the assumption that value is always tied to ownership and individual possession.

Like anthropologists before here, Strathern concurs that gift economies tend to personify objects, meaning that gifts often take on human qualities. But she expands the argument with her interpretation of a "partible" or "multiple" person. This means that one person has different, manifold potential identities and therefore a gift would come to represent one particular trait, or more concretely, that trait in relation to the person receiving the gift. In the Melpa-speaking communities in Papua New Guinea, work comes to represent a commitment between two people. And the object is the outcome and a representation of that relationship. As a result, value exists in the eyes of the beholder because it refers to their particular relation. Value is, thus, relational.

Strathern refers to "making visible" and "giving value" interchangeably. And this practice is the cornerstone of comprehending value in alternative ways. If we want to unlearn value as a ratio of exchange, Strathern, or more concretely, the communities in Mount Hagen present a radical approach to value. Instead of a universal system, each relationship and its gift holds a specific value which is related to the meaning given by a group of people. Strathern uses the notion of relational value to highlight how anthropological analysis can reveal aspects of social life that might otherwise remain obscure. Her work aims to make visible alternative modes of personhood, agency, and creativity that may not be immediately apparent through conventional Western analytical frameworks, but are also fundamental aspects to understand the complex puzzle of exchange beyond the market.

Strathern's work proposes a deep critique of the Western Marxist interpretations of Melanesian societies.[55] For her, referring to notions like "gender," "inequality," and "class," or thinking of labor as a commodified, alienable property imposes hierarchical interpretations on non-Western societies where they may not apply.[56] In Melanesia, artifacts and exchanges reveal rather than obscure human relations, challenging Marxist ideas of alienation and reification,[57] which imply a severance of the relational texture in any exchange.

And how does this relate to blockchain? Distributed ledger technology becomes the tool, using a tokenized system, that could make visible and, therefore, valuable exchanges and relationships that before would fall under the darkness of disparate value systems produced outside the workplace. Blockchain creates a shared infrastructure where both market and nonmarket values can be recognized and exchanged, directly addressing the concerns raised by the theory of value exchange. This means that tokens are relational to the particular community in which they are embedded. This is also why artists are drawn to this space. Beyond using it as a medium, they engage with blockchain as a structural and conceptual proposition. It allows them to prototype new systems of value, authorship, and distribution that resist the extractive economies of the traditional art world. In doing so, they do not simply critique existing models, but also actively build and perform alternatives that foreground collaboration, mutual recognition, and collective agency. Blockchain has the potential to disrupt dominant economic paradigms by offering a system in which value is shaped by the social fabric of communities rather than dictated by external forces, performing value as a relational, community-based practice.

MonedaPAR is an example of a community currency in Argentina that was created in 2017 in response to the country's economic instability. MonedaPAR functions as a mutual credit system in which people can participate after being endorsed by other members of the community, and are able to demonstrate their ability to pay back to the community the same amount initially borrowed. The loans have a zero interest rate, and the exchange offers local produce, courses teaching skills like sports or cooking, help with housework, and secondhand goods. As Gibson-Graham explained, in community economies class politics disappear, the foci for organizing is different, and users are referred to as "prosumers." "All of us need to consume from the community's production, but at the same time we all have something to give to our fellow community members. In a mutual credit system, we can also decide to give value to certain activities that the market usually doesn't remunerate" explains MonedaPAR's website.[58] Here value is allocated to what makes and builds the community; it implies an ethical commitment instead of the paradigm of growth or profit. Working across different cities in the country, the project provides liquidity to a vulnerable section of the population, and becomes a proposal for a decentralized barter system united by a shared goal of cooperation and support.

To rethink value in a non-capitalocentric fashion implies, accordingly, positioning community at the core of the assessment. It is related to the social surplus, which is dedicated "to build[ing] and sustain[ing] the material and cultural infrastructure of the social order. It is thus the potential object of ethical decision and political contestation."[59] Unlike surplus labor, whose appropriation or distribution always entails a class process, social surplus fosters the relationships that make a community. This is what Jean-Luc Nancy called "being-in-common" or the "commonality of being."[60] Therefore reframing value beyond the market is correlated to the particular way that social surplus is used.

The ethical dimension of that decision-making process is guided by a set of diverse, noncapitalist values that drive and perform the various types of community economies. For example, whether a collective action depletes, maintains, or grows the commons plays an enormous role in its determination.[61] Unlike Cartesian ethics, which are embedded in modern capitalist concepts of economy, these are plural systems of embodied ethical practices.[62] These ethical codes of conduct, norms, or virtues are not abstract, disembodied, and *universal*; rather, they are plural practices of ethics that respond to the particularities of each community economy. Accordingly, these ethical decisions come to inhabit, configure, and be performed by bodies who compose the community.[63] This means that each community would adopt different sets of ideals based on distinct notions of responsibility, care, rights, and justice.[64]

In my view, to rethink value is part of the work started by J. K. Gibson-Graham to compose a new language of economic diversity. Value needs to be liberated from the dominance of class relations of surplus appropriation and distribution in order to encompass a broader network of care relationships. These exchanges revolve around socially commensurable transactions that foster social reproduction. Political economist Massimo De Angelis explains that "if we do not ground our critique of mainstream discourse on the problematisation of this law of value, then we will not be able to gain discursive, practice and political autonomy from the interests and value practices of capital."[65] Accordingly, the path toward emancipation from capitalocentric subjugation necessarily entails reconfiguring our relation to value.

Barbara Cueto: Through smart contracts and token design, blockchain gives the possibility of enacting diverse economic systems and practicing new lexicons of economic diversity. For me, the idea of value is always at the core of this process. And, with it, the idea of queering it. To rethink value in a non-capitalocentric fashion would imply to position the community at [the] core of the assessment. That is to say that, it relates to the idea of interdependencies, and making them visible. Here I am thinking of the work of anthropologist Marilyn Strathern who indicates that social relations acquire value through the process of being acknowledged by others. Then, in a blockchain context, where everything can be potentially quantifiable, we would be avoid[ing] the problem of incommensurability of nonmarket transactions. Could we maybe speculate a bit, what would happen if we would overcome this problem?

Katherine Gibson: Many years before we became interested in poststructuralist feminist thinking, Julie and I worked on value theory, and Marxian value theory, trying to look beyond price values to look at relations of surplus value and accumulation, and falling rates of profit in the value sphere, in order to try and understand how capitalist restructuring was taking place. That involves a lot of econometric modeling, using input-output tables moving from the materiality of exchange to what was the actual surplus. And, we felt like it led to a dead end, really. Although it was reflecting the world more accurately in Marxian terms as opposed to price terms, it wasn't telling us anything that people didn't already know. So, it didn't help us predict where the next sector would become in crisis or anything like that. In fact, it became part of an arcane discussion within Marxian theory, as in what's correct and what's not. And what's the best way to measure this and that. So we became less and less interested in those value debates.

I haven't been that involved in trying to reinvent a value. And I'm interested to see the way blockchain is trying to do that, and to what extent [it] is focused on the question of exchange, because it seems to me that [in] the ways in which we talk about community economies, exchange is just one of the many moments of an economy. Production, the access and the negotiation of ownership, the questions of how you save and finance things, etc., [and] the actual exchange moment, which has been focused on commodity exchange, are just some of what an economy is.

To what extent [can] blockchain . . . be used to only focus on those kinds of relationships of exchange versus other things? I'm not sure. I'd be interested to hear what you have to say. But I guess that the theorization of community economies is thinking about the kind of ethical relationships that make up an economy, or that could make up an economy. And those relationships are partly to do with how we regard the others in the process of exchange. Money in formal markets [has] been washing out the social relations of exchange and making it purely calculative. A cold kind of movement of money that's supposed to equilibrate supply and demand, as opposed to a relationship where one

> is looking to the well-being of the other. There are different kinds of sociality and ecological relationships, and I might pay more for it. For instance, do I want to buy this T-shirt knowing that it's based on water extractivism in Mexico? But that's the ethical decision on choice. So that's where this question of interdependency comes into every economic relationship, the same thing with the idea of generation of surplus. So how can blockchain work here? I don't know.
>
> Blockchain is very tied into computer mechanisms and algorithms and so on, which means that it's accessible to a certain proportion of people in the world and not others. But you know, it's obviously something that a lot of people are interested in pursuing and how it relates to our work on community economies is still an open question for me.

Recomposing value as a non-capitalocentric notion is a comprehensive endeavor with profound repercussions on social coordination. If value becomes fluid, responsive, relational, and a diverse non-capitalocentric practice, social life would aim at fostering the being-in-common. These systems of cooperation tacitly emphasize the ethical dimension of the decision-making process on the use of social surplus. At this point, one might argue that blockchain could simply intensify the dominance of financial logics, reducing every relation to an asset that can be accounted. But the more urgent and generative question is: how might blockchain instead be used to support forms of coordination that foreground values not related to the rule of the capital? This is the role that artists take, of unlearning the notion of value beyond the market to rethink the possibilities of blockchain. This exercise is not about reinventing the wheel: community economies have long being active without it and artists have long worked along these lines. But blockchain can potentially create a translocal network of cooperation resisting hegemonic vocabularies of economic domination. If blockchain technology can make visible the connecting threads constructing a community, then blockchains can also tailor the meaning of value to the specificities of a particular community. Value is liberated, free to be adopted in its multiplicity to any postcapitalist project.

MAKE VISIBLE = GIVING VALUE: TOKENS IN SOCIAL PRODUCTION

Unchaining value from the market holds a performative impulse that transforms economic practices into assemblages of ideas, human actors, and more-than-human agencies. Tokens, which are a unique feature of blockchain, are likewise socio-technical assemblages, which connect people while also removing or radically reducing traditional institutions.[66] When tokens are conceived as a substitute apparatus channeling social interaction exceeding the logic of capitalism, the technology can perform multidimensional values and motivations inherent to a diverse P2P economic system. But how?

Tokens are minimal programmable protocols that regulate a P2P network based on a system of value that is shared by all the peers.[67] What was only understood as a monetary feature that took the shape of a Bitcoin can now, as a token, be conceptualized as a whole array of nonmonetary interactions such as sharing, voting, or reputation schemes. It is a mixed asset: part commodity, part currency, part equity, and part unit of distributed governance. The multiple shapes *make visible* and therefore valuable the interdependencies between all subjects in the economic decision-making.[68] That is to say: they allocate worth to non-capitalocentric values that previously remained on the outskirts of the economic systems of neoliberalism.

Tokens hold multiple usages and attributes, and that is why the taxonomy is not clear-cut. I group them into four categories depending on the role of the token's design, identifying purpose, governance, and functional or technical attributes.[69] The first type of tokens is classified by its purpose, such as class (currency, utility, or security), function (asset, usage, or work token), and role (right, value exchange). The second token category relates to what the token effectively represents and how it relates to the governance of the platform and its incentivization. In the third category, tokens are divided by functional attributes, which translates into their spendability, tradability, burnability, expirability, and fungibility.[70] And the fourth category comprises those tokens with technical qualities that refer to their underlying technical layer, such as the protocol or application in which the token is based. Other variations and mixes occur between those categories. In my groupings I purposely decided not to include one token type: kin tokens, whose value is intrinsically related to their capacity of community-making and community-belonging. I will talk more about kin tokens in chapter 3 of this book.

Any community using tokens for their governance can accordingly program and, via smart contracts, tailor their kind of social and economic relations. This reflective potential makes blockchains socially responsive and context-specific. For example, Dayra is a blockchain project operating behind The Question of Funding, a collective of community organizers, artists, and curators in Palestine, who attracted public scrutiny during documenta 15, curated by ruangrupa. The collective's exhibition was vandalized by a Nazi group before the opening, and later its members were criticized as anti-semitic, making it easy to miss the truly transformative potential of their proposal. Dayra is a social blockchain project dedicated to "circulate communal debt within existing trust circles. It allows inter-dependency between different economies in the society through measuring, sharing, and exchanging the value of their local resources as existing wealth in the absence of money."[71] This project is able to provide a structure of exchange for community economies in Palestine, offering a universal measuring tape that can be used to exchange skills, produce, or a location. The possibilities are manifold, and so are their uses. That is how Dayra manages to support a community independently of any monetary exchange. Dayra uses a zero-sum system, which is a win-lose situation, with the initial investment in Dayras (their token) divided between a personal pot and a common one. The personal will hold the same number of validation points to Dayras and, with them, "a member can validate a certain act of sharing by another member, and therefore the system can release the agreed upon Dayras from the member's account to their wallet."[72] A validation point means a fraction of the communal debt, which is shared between all members after enrolling in the project.

Trust is at the core of all of these types of projects. If we want to foster trust, we need to be aware of the social and cultural practice of those communities, which have to be integrated in the (technological) artifact to become, then, a situated technology. In the case of Dayra, the organizers mention as inspiration existing practices of shared debt in Palestine such as Nuqoot, Jama'yeh, and Al Oneh. Nuqoot, as illustration, is a form of communal debt that is paid from one generation to the next for occasions such as a wedding. This system covers the expenses of the newlyweds, who are supposed to pay the debt back to the new generation. Everyone is expected to participate, meaning that Nuqoot shapes an uninterrupted mode of support. If one were to transpose this system to Germany, for example, it wouldn't function because there is no trust in the custom. Therefore, for a technological commons-oriented project to succeed, it must channel existing practices, ideals, and social goals. And this means being aware of the cultural conditions and incorporating social connotations into the design of the collaborations. As a result, this process recasts the technology as an agent of change facilitating autonomous nonmarket production and fosters new social relations focusing on the fostering of their common pool instead.

Blockchain is a "universal, permanent, continuous, consensus-driven, publicly auditable, redundant, record-keeping repository."[73] These public record-keeping features are especially useful, again, when we talk about the commons, both in terms of increasing and enriching the common pool, and as a way to regulate the community and structure its social relations.[74] To start with, tokens can track the behavior of participants: their uses and contributions to the commons. Tokens can also make perceptible involvement in the social aspects that help maintain the community, such as care labor, and thereby facilitate the management of routine tasks. Through tokenization, a community using blockchain can develop a set of rules that will be implemented, evaluated, and, on that account, rewarded, which collaterally transforms the notion of value in a diverse practice. To distribute tokens also facilitates distributing value and incentives in different ways. For example, blockchain researcher David Rozas explains that "they may represent equity, decision-making power, property ownership, or labor certificates" with similar properties as those described by Marx.[75]

These systems encourage alternative relations in a community along with facilitating different approaches to the market. The scope and depth of economic governance is enhanced thanks to new types of coordinating institutions that are native to blockchains.[76] Tokenization could also help with the social organization of the commoners, in terms of measuring their participation in the community, resolving conflicts, and improving the efficacy of the decision-making process. For instance, liquid democracy and quadratic voting are two innovative practices possible in blockchain environments. Liquid democracy "is a way of making collaborative decisions, which does not depend on elected representatives, but rather on the transient delegation of votes."[77] Quadratic voting aims to void the tyranny of the majority by allowing people to express how strongly they feel about an issue rather than just whether they are in favor of or opposed to it; thus, they can allocate more (or less) of their votes to that position.[78] This means that each voter receives a set number of credits/tokens: 100, for example. They can distribute the 100 tokens among the available options however they prefer. A voter may allocate all 100 credits to a single option or divide them among multiple choices, weighting them according to their preferences.

Barbara Cueto: In your opinion, how far are we from the moment when a blockchain product could encompass the ideas of community economies?

Katherine Gibson: I know some of the people involved in the non-fungible tokens, and they've started out of a critical perspective on capitalism, and have an interest in promoting something postcapitalist. But all the mechanisms by which these non-fungible tokens get made and transacted and traded becomes an end in itself. The actual "why you might want to do it" is perhaps less obvious. I think that's one of those byproducts of something new. And perhaps there needs to be another generation where that kind of technique is embedded in something where people have a clear idea of exactly why they want to do this trading, and at what point would they pull it out, and put it into currency that they could actually build a community center or a co-housing establishment or whatever goal of producing, and getting involved in this kind of thing.

I also have to acknowledge that in much of my research I was cautious when talking about the emancipatory potential of blockchain. One of the main takeaways of a discursive program I curated at the Van Abbemuseum in the Netherlands about the politics and blockchain was the importance of the community and its internal dynamics in hard-coding a foreign system of rules. One of the speakers in this program, activist and artist Larisa Blazic urged us to go back to basics, to see how the technology could address issues like poverty, while also reflecting on the lack of developers with an ethos that would help solve those kinds of problems. To her, the problem lies in the lack of idealism within technological development. Similarly, another participant, media theorist Shintaro Miyazaki, held that "most of the blockchain projects are pursuing a sort of liberal Fata Morgana, building on ideas such as value contracts, secure ownership, trust, or even price and markets." But, he asked, "who needs that?"[79] For Miyazaki, it is more important to work on the means of communication, protocols, and rules, how things get decided in general, and he asked, why should we use digital technologies for that? I would argue that if we do not engage with the technology at this point in time, when it is still in development, one cannot but renounce the possibility of another internet being possible and, with it, the potential of using this technology for social change.

On the same panel, curator Daphne Dragona pointed out a problem of ownership, noting that "blockchain is based on transparencies and decentralisation, but it is also being used by companies and the market. And like with any technology, it depends in whose hands it is."[80] As is true of any technological apparatus, blockchain is not positive by default; it depends on the uses that it is put to. If we abandon this conversation about the social potential of blockchain technology, we all know very well how neoliberalism could swallow up everything to the benefit of the wealthiest one percent. I still think that there is still (perhaps a small) chance of success. And that's why blockchain technology's world-building ability could help, and how artists help see its radical potential.

BLOCKCHAIN AS A SITE FOR PLACE-BASED POLITICS

The economic geographer Doreen Massey suggested that space is not a mere container for social relations; on the contrary, social relations are constitutive of space and place.[81] Reciprocally, places are composed by their socio-economies and their relations to other places too. Massey argues that "if space is indeed the product of interrelations, then it must be predicated upon the existence of plurality."[82] I argue that any digital space is, thus, an expansion of physical places, and can likewise be shaped by an ecology of actors that include digital, nonhuman, and human relations. Places are the locus of possibility, where worldviews are materialized and, with them, the knowledges and subjectivities.[83] Blockchain acts in the same manner, and represents a hybrid space for the multiplicity of subjectivities of the online and offline, translocal communities that inhabit it.

Barbara Cueto: If squatting is an analog form of activism, and blockchain is the newest version of digital activism, what is the common thread between the two movements?

Geert Lovink: I don't feel the tension so much between the analog in the physical world and the digital. But there is an issue about the traditional space becoming so expensive. And this is the difference between then and now. It is not the technology. There's an overestimation about the technologies being radically different back then. People in the 1970s had to move to the suburbs, they wanted to have more space, and it was affordable. That's not a break. The break really comes in the late 1990s as a result of privatization, and the process of gentrification. Now it is creating both digital nomads and refugees. Right at this moment, hundreds of millions of people in the world are on the move for whatever reason. And they are all on the move with the digital

> technologies. This kind of exodus out of very expensive real estate is something we should really start to think more about. We could say that the blockchain is also anticipating it or facilitating it.

The heterogeneity of the compositions of blockchain facilitates hybrid spaces where community economies of any type can flourish. When one hears about blockchains, it is often in the context of DeFi (decentralized finance), which focuses on decentralizing and optimizing traditional financial systems for efficiency and profit. Often DeFi is about removing intermediaries, which many crypto-libertarians consider a natural extension of their core values. In contrast, the ReFi (regenerative finance) ecosystem is a movement and a set of blockchain-based financial practices designed to address global environmental, social, and economic challenges. Unlike traditional finance, which often prioritizes profit over ecological or social well-being, ReFi aims to create systems that are regenerative, such as systems restoring ecosystems, empowering communities, and promoting long-term sustainability. This is how blockchain-based projects could update what Gibson-Graham calls social surplus, since the core of ReFi projects entails an ethical decision-making process, which generates a type of surplus value that usually falls through the cracks of traditional economic ventures. It also exemplifies how the Web3 ecosystem can also be understood as a space for place-based politics. GainForest.Earth is an example of decentralized, technology-driven ecological conservation. By combining blockchain, AI, remote sensing, and community governance, GainForest.Earth creates a transparent and equitable system where local communities are paid for verified environmental stewardship. The project's use of smart contracts and impact certificates ensures trust, accountability, and financial sustainability, while its open-source tools and participatory approach empower frontline stewards to lead global conservation efforts. GainForest.Earth provides a terrain for place-based politics, as the social relations created through this decentralized technology constitute a hybrid location that lives both in the collective imaginary of the people partaking in it, as well as in the multiple locations across the world where the project takes root. Blockchains enable and activate a community to develop their own postcapitalist proposition.

In these kinds of ReFi projects one can see how diverse non-capitalocentric values constitute the social surplus, which then can be implemented at the level of code, constructing alternative spaces of resistance. Gender and sustainability scholar Wendy Harcourt highlighted that place-based politics are related to reappropriation, reconstruction, and reinvention of practices and possibilities.[84] The blockchain ecosystem can, in the same way, be appropriated, reconstructed, and reinvented to successfully support the experimentation to forge the political project embedded in the multiple compositions of community economies. Whether digital or not, "places act as prisms that refract global economic and governance structures, bending and shaping them in ways that make sense within the politics of particular sites and in different communities."[85] Therefore, as will be further explained in chapter 3, I take blockchain as a site for place-based politics that can give rise to counter-hegemonic systems adapted to the granular necessities of a community.

Decentralized ledger technology can therefore provide a space for the diverse understandings of value that overcome subjugation to capitalocentrism. The potential of blockchain is used in almost opposite ways in DeFi and ReFi. This not only expresses the different perspective in each community, but also implies that the technology can *stage* any social imaginary. This is where artists intervene: not as developers or investors, but as world-builders. They approach the technology not to serve capital, but to shape it into vessels for their own visions. Each blockchain configuration becomes a speculative architecture, a crystallization of a possible future, a tentative path toward collective emancipation. But before we continue, I need to stress that blockchain's emancipatory potential is not associated with capitalism or anticapitalism. If we only think in these terms, we would miss its truly radical potential. What matters is blockchain's plasticity: its capacity to be bent, retooled, and repurposed. Blockchain is a technology of composition. It can be rewritten, forked, rerouted. It invites us to imagine economic forms untethered from accumulation, infrastructures rooted in trust, and communities bound by affinities rather than transactions. Again, we need to think across binary oppositions. Blockchain can help us queer economic languages and, thus, enunciate a site of economic diversity. There is a recursive movement: blockchain can transform the notion of value into a diverse practice and, at the same time, the diverse economic systems transform blockchain into a tool for social organizing. And artists help visualize this movement.

Still, we must be honest. Blockchain is no free space. It is forged within the apparatus of late capitalism, shaped by its logics, haunted by its imperatives. It rides the waves of speculation but these fluctuations are not the concern of this book. The market is not the protagonist here. This is a book about imagination as a political force. About wresting technology from the grip of the market. About reclaiming code as common ground. About artists who do not merely reflect the world, but who forge new ones. Blockchain, in this light, becomes not a tool of capital, but a medium for dreaming otherwise.

Like Harcourt's politics of space,[86] then, blockchain is a digital place with political power, a structure and a practice that can be continuously reappropriated, reconstructed, and reinvented. By doing so, blockchain configurations set at the margins of economic discourses facilitate vibrant new understandings of economy, politics, and social relations. As Vitalik Buterin, co-creator of Ethereum, puts it, "Blockchains are . . . Lego Mindstorms for building economic and social institutions."[87] Hence, if we consider distributed ledger technology only as a financial tool, we also miss its radical potential. Blockchain is a hyperpolitical tool that can be put to work on any political project. And that's why we need to repoliticize and appropriate it to develop our own project of autonomy.

As a result, distributed ledger technology holds the potential to challenge capital markets and commodity exchange because it can provide an infrastructure that can support commons-oriented economies.[88] The ReFi ecosystem is not a mere economic alternative, it is a proposal for how blockchain technology can be mobilized to support sustainable, regenerative, and socially oriented practices. These initiatives challenge conventional notions of value, introducing forms of social surplus and collective benefit that resist extraction-driven economic models. In doing so, they also contribute to reshaping blockchain itself; not only as a technical infrastructure, but also as a space for place-based politics and for reimagining value beyond purely financial terms. By doing this, blockchain successfully challenges two concepts that are fundamentally associated with our current idea of value: the mechanism of supply and demand, and property. Blockchain provides scaffolding to maintain a network of peers cooperating on a voluntary basis. This means that supply and demand does not have much influence on the output, which can be freely used and reused by the community. Like any other CBPP (commons-based peer production), it sustains liberal licensing schemes, like copyright, for instance. This context facilitates innovation and enhances creativity. Media theorist Yochai Benkler, firm opponent to this type of legislation, affirms: "Freedom to operate is more important than power to appropriate."[89]

Lastly, blockchain stretches the idea of property, as the system is collectively owned and controlled, and can endow property rights "independently of any legal institutions."[90] I want to point out that this is not like another nightmare coming from what we happily titled the sharing economy in the early 2010s. This is not like Uber or Airbnb but more like a cooperative system. Value, in this case, is allocated to access, not ownership. It solves the prosperity paradox, distributing wealth via value creation in participatory systems of production, and value participation through distributed ownership.[91]

Blockchain can generate a shift from exclusivity of the ownership of the means of production, to a collective management of resources. That is, from hierarchical command of labor and surplus value, to flat hierarchies where permissionless contributions create shared value and resources that can be reused. These possibilities are not merely theoretical. For instance, another project, Gitcoin, provides a platform for funding public goods through quadratic funding and community-led allocation. It demonstrates how collective contributions create a pool of shared resources, flattening hierarchies of funding power. In it, wealth is not redistributed by a central authority but allocated by *crowd preference*. In such projects blockchain becomes a tool that could facilitate what the collective Telekomunisten (Dmytri Kleiner and Baruch Gottlieb) called Transvestment, a process that describes the transfer of value from one modality to another—in this case, from capitalocentrism to community economies. Naturally, Transvestment also entails a political transformation.

DECENTRALIZATION AS A POLITICAL TACTIC

To understand blockchain as a political terrain we need to take a step backward and understand the very essence of its architecture: decentralization. This is in itself already a political gesture, not just a type of architecture, not just a type of organization. Decentralization has been described by Ben Waters as "power, control, access, or ownership, as they are spread across multiple actors, points, or nodes comprising a network. It is reflected and manifested in various architectures, collectives, and frameworks."[92] Why is decentralization so important? Benkler clarifies that decentralized systems have the capacity to provide self-determination over the communicative environment.[93] The users are no longer passive, but active agents within the network, selecting from the different sources as well as securing a censorship-free setting. A decentralized communicative environment, consequently, cannot be co-opted because all parts have stakes in its protection. Thus, collective action also procures a secure system for the group as a whole. This agency within the system bestows all agents with enhanced criticality, as they are contributing to the development of an analytical worldview and culture. Similarly, when we talk about decentralized protocols, they also act in opposition to restricting outlooks and constrictive relations supported by centralized infrastructures.

Decentralization is not only a way of systematically arranging something: it is also a response to the growing mistrust in government and the accumulation of power in the digital terrain, because it goes against the existing dynamics that tend toward a greater centralization and the stabilization of power.[94] Decentralization promotes personal autonomy and collective self-governance, which implies regaining agency over the system and a collective desire to envision an alternative future. As criticality is enhanced in decentralized systems, the desire for autonomy rises. This situation triggers new ways of self-organization that carry worldviews, prospects, and attitudes that are introduced through a newfound sense of self-determination. Decentralization provides alternative forms of coordination along with promoting values according to the ethics of each community. Communities of digital artists, for instance, are spread across the internet, but unite online in platforms like Discord, which is a decentralized communication platform, to share the same values, desires, and ambitions. Decentralization becomes an organizing mechanism to sustain social structures based on perspectives that escape the mainstream.

In the digital realm, decentralized infrastructures often function as P2P collaborative systems. These are configurations in which individuals, united by shared values and goals, voluntarily participate in collective endeavors. Such systems give rise to digital communities shaped not by institutional authority but by a mutual commitment to cooperation and trust. Examples such as the previously explained community currency MonedaPAR and Dayra illustrate how these infrastructures operate in practice. Another example is Nettime, initiated by Club Berlin for the 1995 Venice Biennale. Nettime is a P2P platform where early internet adopters, artists, and theorists come together to engage in critical dialogue around networked cultures, media policies, and activist tactics. In chapter 2 I will argue that this project extends the legacy of institutional critique into the networked digital environment, where cultural production and political agency are deeply intertwined. These communities are articulated through specific shared values, where P2P acts as a relational dynamic of human interaction, and where all parts have the potential to act as equals based on trust.[95] As media theorists and commons experts Michel Bauwens and Alekos Pantazis explain, this feature unavoidably conveys a nonhierarchical network where "peers are interconnected nodes holding interchangeable roles."[96]

P2P and CBPP are similar concepts that I will use interchangeably for the sake of clarity. Economist and commons researcher Elinor Ostrom clarifies that CBPP provides social capital to the user, since these values are related to how the social surplus is used in the community.[97] These values, which Elinor Ostrom calls transcendental, are opposite to market-translatable principles because they cannot be converted into economic assets, as they are not quantifiable. They are non-capitalocentric values, which means they refer to ethical ideals. Primavera de Filippi, an expert in commons and blockchain, explains that this value type is "related to a normatively structured worldview, whose fulfilment depends on people's ability to live well according to the horizons of the community at stake."[98] Therefore, they are a representation of the underlying values of a community and are intrinsic to P2P cooperation systems, making those systems a form of emancipation from digital hegemonic power. This is, therefore, a political attitude that stimulates structures with alternative social production. As human geographer Paul Chatterton asserts, "The common is full of productive moments of resistance that create new vocabularies, solidarities, social and spatial practices and relations and repertoires of resistance."[99] P2P communities foster new forms of dissent that subvert centralized control systems by following diverse, non-capitalocentric values.

Enspiral is a network of social entrepreneurs and activists from New Zealand that coordinates its activities through open-source, decentralized collaborative tools such as Loomio (for deliberation) and Cobudget (for resource allocation). Enspiral's approach does not depend on distributed ledgers. Its decentralization is enacted through participatory digital infrastructures that are transparent, inclusive, and community-driven. Precisely because it is not technologically bound to blockchain, Enspiral demonstrates that decentralization is not a matter of code alone but also of governance, culture, and shared ethical commitments. Its model shows how collective decision-making and budgeting can be structured around trust, openness, and solidarity rather than competitive accumulation.

To develop alternative infrastructures against the concentration of power in digital corporations is not only an act of resistance but also a practice of imagination. Projects such as Enspiral, MonedaPAR, and Nettime demonstrate that decentralization is not merely a counterforce to centralized authority, but a way of cultivating new modes of collaboration grounded in trust and shared responsibility. Within this lineage, blockchain extends an ongoing project: resisting hegemonic systems of power concentration. Decentralization equips communities with the capacity to shape their own conditions of cooperation, to articulate values beyond capital, and to enact forms of governance that reflect their collective imagination. Rather than standing alone, blockchain carries forward a shared desire for autonomy, extending earlier efforts to resist concentrated power. It embodies the ongoing search for alternative infrastructures of cooperation, where communities can imagine and enact different ways of living together.

ISSUES RELATED TO BLOCKCHAIN REGULATORY FRAMEWORKS

Blockchain technology is a powerful machinery whose effects are far from being clear, as mass adoption is still distant on our horizon. Although I position my investigation as a call for action and a pledge to optimism, lex cryptographica, the private regulatory frameworks that operate on each blockchain, can likewise have the reverse effect: to exacerbate control and generate a dystopia of algorithmic governmentality. It can both lead to a process of reconcentration of power, as well as trigger collateral forms of oppression related to the quality of the rules.

The values and rules implemented in the governance structure of a DAO are enforced by the underlying protocol of a blockchain-based network. This means that they are in legal limbo as they do not comply with the law: they exist in a para-legality. While this process can potentially readdress hierarchies of power by acknowledging interdependencies, it can also stimulate a translocation of power from the government to other agents or technocratic actors.[100] Instead of replacing forever the hegemonic systems of power such as banks or politicians, one could be exchanging them for another technical set of likely heteronormative male coders or computer scientists. Or even worse, it could add another layer of complexity. For example, in the case of data stewardship, governments would likely continue to be accountable if there were a failure or a problem with the quality of the data, which would require the reintermediation of the role of government.[101]

The problem of accountability is not the only one. Joy Buolamwini, a researcher in the now disappeared MIT Media Lab's Civic Media group, conducted a brilliant experiment: she used a white mask to expose skin type and gender bias in commercial AI products from IBM, Microsoft, and Amazon. Blockchain, like any other technology, could also replicate bias, influence, or partisan politics,[102] or it could generate oligarchies.[103] As philosopher Oliver Leistert acknowledges, although technology can be empowering, it cannot, alone, modify power relations and improve the distribution of power.[104] More likely than not, it will bring power to the Vectorialist Class, which media theorist McKenzie Wark defines as those who own the communication vectors and who shape the circuits whereby power and wealth are distributed in the digital realm to the owners' benefit.[105]

There are another set of issues related to lex cryptographica because of its normative tempo, which is ex ante. Once a set of rules is decided, there is limited influence over the smart contracts, which will enforce these norms without discretion. Consequently, the normative system becomes ex ante rather than ex post, which makes them more difficult to break, but it's also harder to define exceptions.[106] Due to the apparent complexity of nonhuman agency, it could also raise a problem of accountability, which might lead to privatized entities taking advantage of those obscurities.[107] In extreme cases, it can also turn into a Techno-Leviathan situation. As the users comply blindly to the authoritarian rules of the smart contract without the possibility of change, they also lose their agency. Although a Leviathan could have been decided democratically, once it assumes power it can become totalitarian. As a result, lex cryptographica can convey a regime of continuous and granular control based on ex-ante regulations that will substitute the traditional ex-post mechanism of punishment. Therefore, control moves away from governments to dwell in private structures where regulation is so prevalent that it modifies the behaviors and activities of the individuals in the public and private spheres in accordance with the pre-set rules.[108]

The transformation into an ex-ante regulatory regime can also precipitate a hyperfinancialized system due to overtokenization. Tokens have different uses and, inherently, they can also be accumulated and, again, trigger new cycles of appropriation and extraction. It could also exacerbate the capitalization of the attention economy. Distributed ledger technology can timestamp and transparently indicate the transfer and usage of whatever asset is regulated with it. Based on that information, a smart contract can also modulate its uses very specifically. Web3 researcher Laura Lotti suggests it can "produce more virulent and capillary forms of extraction in the attention economy, thereby reinforcing familiar dynamics."[109] This modulated use-time regimen surpasses ownership and could exploit our attention timespans, which can be properly assessed and profited from.

These risks need to be taken into account as a way to avoid the perils of ex-ante control diminishing the agency over the system by community peers. Inevitably, blockchain technology has both great potential for emancipation, but also for curbing autonomy. Running fast toward implementation means potentially falling into the same problems we had before, leaving it up to the Vectorialist Class to decide the uses. This group would likely repeat problems that we all know too well from the Web 2.0: replicating bias and allocating black-boxed decision-making capacity to a rather white heteronormative male fraction of the world. Blockchain research needs to concentrate on what happens before, to find out how communities work to respect them and create a network of trust in the technology as a collective good. Activating a technological artifact as a regulatory framework in a community needs to respond to the specific qualities of that collective. A system of tokenized incentives could lead to the formalization of social relations, which could have ripple effects. It can make explicit formal relations that were previously personal and implicit, for example, and devalue the contributions based on altruism or social responsibilities.[110] It can, as Jerry Muller explained, result in the adaptation of the contributions to the predefined categories, which could disincentivize innovation and creativity.[111] It can provoke a tendency toward accommodation or less reflexivity over time as a consequence of automation.[112] And it can overtly trigger an internalization of the rules. As we know, a ranking system could also be seen as an internal reputation contest. As artist Gary Zhexi Zhang admitted, "You need affordances for coordination but the kind of bonds and basic relationship between people are essential."[113] Naturally, there are examples of social cooperation off-chain; for example, Broodfonds or cooperatives.[114] But, as Zhang noted, those are monocultures, where it is much easier for people to agree on basic things when they have already excluded people who are not like them. That is of course true. But what I would like to stress is that blockchain gives different communities the opportunity to design a type of governance aligned to their desires and goals. This does not mean that all would agree with the same system of penalties and rewards, but a certain group of people would. For them, the technology would become a social apparatus that would support their *own* project of autonomy.

USING BLOCKCHAINS AS POLITICAL TOOLS

The allegedly disruptive potential of blockchain is a recurrent topic in a wide range of literature, exposing its radical transformative capacity in terms of economics, politics, and governance.[115] I propose two complementary perspectives—micro and macro—to unfold this issue. The micro perspective refers to the relation between blockchain and Jacques Rancière's Redistribution of the Sensible, proposed by researcher Jaya Brekke.[116] And built upon this knowledge, the macro perspective considers the potential role of blockchain coordination in relation to social movements by analyzing the work of sociologist Manuel Castells.[117]

Micropolitics: Overcoming Neutrality

More often than not, mathematics and code seem to be elevated to languages with a universal value of neutrality, far from mischievous forms of interpretation. Nonetheless, code not only describes but also simultaneously executes.[118] Therefore, it has direct effects, which inevitably encompass political consequences.

To untangle this notion, I considered Jaya Brekke's doctoral dissertation "Disassembling the Trust Machine," which investigates the complex relations that condition blockchain politically by looking from within the technology.[119] She denounces the impossibility of impartiality, and describes three layers where power and the political play out on blockchain: first, the protocol, where politics are encoded immanently; second, the governance layer, which is related to the explicit political decisions taken in the development of the protocol; and third, the interfaces, as in the actual effects of the political in relation to the different contexts and conditions.[120] There are also external relations that influence the political overtones of the technology and its perception to the end user in different modes. On a very basic level, some aspects are determined by mathematical dynamics, or the capacity of fiber optics;[121] on a human level, our styles of semantic interpretation cannot accurately grasp machine-learning algorithms.[122] Even when those algorithms are graspable, they also need to come from contexts that are reliable and secure, because as explained before, the community needs to trust the technology, which needs to reflect their customs in return. In addition, the development is also guided by different technical, geographical, political, and legal systems, which intersect and mobilize specific agendas and purposes, as media theorist Benjamin Bratton describes in *The Stack: On Software and Sovereignty*.[123]

Therefore, politics runs through every single aspect of the composition of blockchain. The technology is not neutral but rather, innately political both in its technical aspects and in the way that is activated, as it is situated in the techno-political complex. It can, therefore, reproduce (or debunk) the structures of power that it is subjugated by and, as such, it represents the possibility of dissensus. Dissensus is an intense sense of disruption that not only modifies power dynamics in a given social order, but also runs deeply, transforming the sensible. Rancière describes it as a kind of status quo, or "common sense" that articulates what is right or not, both in actions and subjects.[124] The sensible organizes reality spatially and experientially, and it translates into norms, culture, ways of speaking, laws, and politics. In the same vein, the radical potential of blockchain relies on its capacity to disrupt the given order—namely, the systems implied in capitalism[125]—and, as such, it opens a path toward diverse economies described by J. K. Gibson-Graham.[126]

Macropolitics: Blockchain as a Counterpower Tool

Brekke's argument looks inward and pivots on why the technology is immanently political. Complementary to her approach and built upon this knowledge, my position takes a macro perspective, looking from the outside into the technology to understand how to use it *politically*. My argument acknowledges, therefore, blockchain's political nuances and repoliticizes it as a form of voicing dissent. To navigate this change of perspective, I considered new social movement theory, in particular Castells's *Networks of Outrage and Hope*, as a way to understand the composition of the communities that could find their path toward emancipation using blockchain.[127] I believe the structural versatility and the manifold uses of its affordances can respond to the polymorphic compositions and desires from new communities born out of previous social movements. It is not that blockchain infrastructures will channel all social movements; rather, the technology provides a structure for social organizing that reacts to the particularities of each community.

Barbara Cueto: Long-term strategic thinking has a lot to do with the political agency. Whereas tactical media [a form of digital activism] operates in the present, Critical Blockchain Art can prefigure an alternative. Could this different temporal matrix affect the agency of Critical Blockchain Art?

Geert Lovink: Blockchain infrastructure can facilitate and provoke new forms of intervention. And interventions in the long term will only be possible if there is an underlying structure. In the past, social infrastructure was defined differently; before World War II people were primarily thinking of the party, the trade union, and related infrastructures, like the labor movement or the feminist movement. After the war, these types of traditional infrastructures started to decline. My generation faced the crisis of the party and the union, and all the traditional forms. We then started to figure out what is the underlying infrastructure for an autonomous social movement or a rainbow of different social movements. New generations would call it intersectional. We never used that word, but it describes it very precisely. Intersectionality is something that exists between people and initiatives, like strong networks that care and support each other. In my understanding, blockchain is the underlying economic and financial support system to achieve that.

The technology is particularly fitting given the composition of the social base and the meshwork-like organization of social movements from the 2010s onward, understood here as forms of collective action held together by ongoing relations, shared practices, and mutual dependencies rather than central leadership or fixed hierarchies. The year 2008 marks both an end and a beginning. With the collapse of Lehman Brothers, the global economy was shaken to its core. To many, what followed was not simply a shift in economic policy but a collapse of faith in the promise of endless growth. The ensuing years of austerity revealed a deeper collective despair, sparking a wave of political unrest across the globe. From Tahrir Square to Puerta del Sol, from Occupy Wall Street to Gezi Park, new movements emerged, horizontally organized and deeply networked, drawing power from the connective capacities of the internet. It was a moment when digital infrastructures offered not only tools for coordination but also a sense of shared possibility. The internet became more than a medium; it became a terrain for action, and solidarity.

At the same time, many artists developed socially engaged practices that responded directly to these political conditions.

Technology was not simply a subject of inquiry but also a material to be worked with, a structure to be exposed, and a means to forge new forms of relation. Projects such as Zach Blas's *Facial Weaponization Suite* confronted biometric surveillance by producing masks that confounded facial recognition systems, transforming technologies of control into instruments of resistance. These works exemplify a radical approach to art making, where aesthetic practice becomes a mode of political intervention and where technology is repurposed to question systems of power, enable collective agency, and propose alternative ways of being in the world.

In the years that followed, many of these movements lost political momentum, but their energy, or perhaps their soul, continues to resonate in the radical uses of technology. This was not the end of socially engaged artistic practices that critically explored digital infrastructures. Rather, the conversations deepened and the questions shifted. While the internet played a crucial role in enabling the coordination and expression of those earlier movements, blockchain technology represents something more structurally ambitious. It is not only the infrastructure but also the conceptual core of an emerging paradigm. As activist and scholar Emiliano Treré has observed, blockchain can function as a rhetorical device. Technologies are not only used to achieve political ends, but are also deployed discursively to open new horizons of meaning and possibility. It is in this dual role that blockchain becomes a tool for radical imagination. When we think with it, rather than merely about it, we begin to construct alternative social imaginaries. Artists have embraced this potential, not by celebrating the technology uncritically, but by probing its contradictions, limitations, and potential. Their work often treats blockchain as a conceptual material, engaging with its technical properties as well as its symbolic and social dimensions. From speculative currencies and autonomous collectives to experiments in decentralized governance and value redistribution, artists use blockchain to model systems that challenge extractive economies and reimagine ownership, labor, and exchange. In doing so, they continue the unfinished labor of previous movements. They tested how technologies might serve not only critique but also collective creation, not only disruption but also care. Decentralized ledger technologies provide not just new tools; they also offer new conditions for imagining how we might live and organize together.

Barbara Cueto: Tactical media is a form of activism. If we think of long-term strategic thinking in social movements, what do we need to consider? What could be the role of blockchain? Why did you become interested in it in the first place?

Geert Lovink: This goes back to a desire, a demand, a requirement, already very strong in the movements of the 1970s and 1980s, namely, that if you want autonomy, you have to really organize it yourself. You have to take full responsibility. You can't just demand autonomy halfway, there's no such thing. There is a question of finance. If you create an autonomous practice, this is the first thing you're going to ask yourself: what is the revenue model. If you don't, the initiative will die a week later or a few months later. The question of autonomy is a long-term one. It's really related to building up autonomous infrastructure that will sustain and that will facilitate and reproduce, and there's also an element of care. Short term is the protest, the revolt, the reaction coming together. But that's not what we're talking about. We're talking really about infrastructures that will sustain this.

New social movements are rooted in the rejection of contemporary oppressive structures, a gesture that also lies at the origin of blockchain technology. Its foundational white paper

"Bitcoin: A Peer-to-Peer Electronic Cash System" (2008) called for disintermediation and offered an alternative to dominant regulatory and financial systems. In both contexts, collective action foregrounds the constructed nature of the world and the power structures embedded within it. It also opens up the possibility of building alternatives through shared agency. According to new social movement theory, the social base of such movements is heterogeneous. There is no single status or identity that unites the collective. Rather, individuals align themselves with a movement because they recognize a resonance between their own values and the movement's goals.[128] These values are often in deep contradiction with the systems that currently hold power.

What defines these polymorphic groups is not a common identity, shared mythology, or unified narrative. They are not primarily organized around identity politics but around a shared urgency to reimagine existing structures. The cohesion of these collectives emerges through constant online engagement through tweets, Facebook posts, Telegram groups, and other forms of distributed interaction. This digital participation does more than organize; it creates a sense of kinship and helps sustain political momentum in physical spaces. As Claus Pias notes, the endurance of these movements depends on technological mediation, immediate connectivity, and affective bonds formed through communication.[129] In this way, technological infrastructures not only support mobilization, but also become integral to the formation and continuity of the movement itself.

This fluid internal architecture is useful to understanding how distributed ledger technology can provide an adaptable social coordination in accordance to the plurality of a group, which is united by the affective connection and shared goals. Sociologist Alberto Melucci explains that these movements "invoke solidarity, make manifest a conflict, and entail a breach of the limits of compatibility of the system within which the action takes place."[130] Alberto Melucci's theory is based on an assumed overcoming of industrial capitalism and, with it, the old worker-based constituencies for social activism. Essentially, these are replaced in the post-Fordist society with the affiliation with collectives, which differs from classical organizations such as unions or political parties. In 1983 Castells had already concluded that the demands of urban protest movements focused on the forms of collective consumption provided by the state, as these movements aimed at challenging the capitalist logic of surplus value extraction by prioritizing the provision of use value in a community context. Naturally, this also ties back to J. K. Gibson Graham's diverse economic systems overcoming class politics as well as the focus on social surplus. For example, the demonstrations of Indignados in Spain led to forms of diverse economic systems called Grupos de Consumo. Inspired by cooperativism, these P2P networks buy and sell groceries to local producers, with the goal of offering fair prices to the whole community. There is a spirit of political resistance, acting as an alternative to an unfair system and a continuation of the anti-establishment movement before them.

These social movements raise awareness and coordinate the protests using a meshwork system. They are nonlinear, rhizomatic structures, where elements are linked together through strong mutual relations. The term "meshwork" comes from digital technologies, which define a local network topology in which the infrastructure nodes connect directly, dynamically, and nonhierarchically to self-organize and self-configure. It works analogously in activism, enabling P2P contributions to support the entire network, both online and offline. These systems bypass hierarchies of power, procuring informal ways of decentralization, and were originally designed to overcome crisis situations[131] like uprisings, or as a way to avoid control in totalitarian regimes.[132] Now, thanks to blockchain, this mode of organizing can be formalized on a code level.

Barbara Cueto: Do you think that tactical media would have resisted the current tyranny of becoming viral?

Geert Lovink: Virality is itself a 1990s notion, because it is related to the rhizome, something that grows in different directions, and you can't really see, it goes viral. It is an archetypical metaphor for networking. What we would have opposed is the dictatorship of gathering likes and followers just for the sake of it. The ultimate aim of the intervention wasn't to scale up. The idea was more like a gift to the world. Nowadays we're in a different world and things do scale up. If we look at #metoo, BlackLivesMatter, or the protest against the war in Gaza, these are movements created by social media platforms, depending on corporate filters and algorithms that shape both internal and external forms of communication. Is there something beyond? In the case of Extinction Rebellion, it already operates differently. They utilize social media, but they're not a product of it, nor do they live off it. They use the success in social media for self-organization, or PR to some extent, but it's not their dominating mode of organization.

Meshworking coordination constitutes an attempt to transpose the concept of open-source cooperation in the physical world.[133] In both cases, there is a common pool of resources, where everyone could easily join and participate.[134] The value of the network increases the more people participate and contribute. For instance, during the protests in Hong Kong in 2019, the movement had different Telegram groups: one for gear, another to organize traffic and rideshares, another for tracking policemen and activity. In these channels one could provide helmets or gas masks, offer a free car ride, or inform users about a police officer being violent at the metro station.

In this way, the movement seamlessly moved across the hyperpoliced city. Their slogan became "Be Water, my Friend," after the famous Hong Kong actor Bruce Lee. It was through technological mediation, immediate connectivity, and affective connection that the movement managed to continue for months, and posed a serious threat to mainland China's government. Although repression won the battle, this David-Goliath situation was only possible because of the impeccable meshworking coordination.

Although this system of organization has proven its efficiency in recent years, I am sure that many of you have experienced tedious, never-ending assemblies. It is important to remark on the need to develop structures that also deal with community internalities such as decision-making mechanisms, forms of internal organization, and the division of tasks. If we think of movements like Gezi (Istanbul) or Indignados (Spain), the lack of conflict resolution or a decision-making process aggravated the incapacity to secure a political standpoint in spite of a massive following and international repercussions. Both movements were unable to envisage a solution or submit a proposal to government. Blockchain affordances could potentially solve many of these issues through smart contracts and token design. Although many threats might stem from automating these processes, movements could also scale up. However, as Zeynep Tufekci points out, gaining trust in a community is a process that needs communal activities, since new members can learn the ways of working and decision-making through practice. This means that internalities cannot disappear completely, but can only be streamlined to improve the resilience of the movement as a whole.[135]

Blockchain is a site for place-based politics that conveys a new type of dissent, not only because of the technological possibilities, but also because blockchain is heir to these social movements, following the same lineage of disaffection and challenge to the status quo while catering to the heterogeneity of the social base. This desire is integral to the social imagination ingrained in blockchain, which strives to collectively compose opportunities to counter today's transgressions. Blockchain's digital infrastructure is responsive to the values that the New Social Movements put forward, providing a space of possibility where they can flourish based on technology that represents noncompliance with the hierarchies and regulatory principles of the networks of power. At the same time, blockchain turns into an institutional technology that channels the goals of preceding social movements in three ways: first, it offers a communicative environment that is decentralized and uncensored; second, it formalizes the decision-making processes of the assemblies in occupied spaces into a full governance system articulated through smart contracts; and third, it catalyzes the values of a commonality into a transparent, community blockchain-governance structure. By formalizing it, distributed ledger technology can also complete the process of queering economic languages. It solidifies the practice of making visible ethical values and the social interdependencies through a tokenized system that endows them with worth, as Strathern explained.[136]

The social movements come to be spheres of alternative social production within the participating agents, generating a sense of political belonging, which creates a common identity and authority for acting politically.[137] Evidently, this kinship comes from a shared particular value system that is put to the fore in a prefigurative way. Prefiguration refers to the act of representing something in advance to show or suggest that a certain event or state will occur in the future. Activists practice direct democracy, cooperation, and egalitarianism within their groups to demonstrate and build the world they wish to create. Prefiguration is considered an approach, a method, and a commitment to creating, testing, and implementing more democratic structures, forms of organizing and decision-making, new economic models, and ways of relating to each other. While not a new practice, prefiguration has been both an important exercise and a popular analytical lens of alter-globalization movements, Occupy Wall Street, and other groups and movements from across the world that emerged thereafter.[138] The tactics are, concretely, practices such as egalitarian decision-making,[139] voluntary and nonprofit proceedings, decentralized organization, and efforts to fight against discrimination and oppressive social forms.[140] Prefiguration as an act of speculation has not escaped critique. Its practices often flourish in small circles but prove hard to sustain or expand, where consensus risks paralyzing action or muting dissent. Movements that cling to high ethical standards set themselves up for frustration, since remaining untouched by state, market, or other communities is rarely possible. At times, prefigurative groups may even reproduce the hierarchies they aim to abolish, or see their radical edge weaken when their methods become mainstream as they are taken up and institutionalized elsewhere.

Artists have long engaged in prefigurative practices, using their work and modes of organization to model alternative ways of living and relating. The DAOWO (Decentralised Autonomous Organisation With Others) series, initiated by Furtherfield, exemplifies this impulse by staging collaborative experiments that rethink art economies and collective authorship through blockchain. These initiatives do more than critique existing infrastructures; they enact speculative proposals for how cultural production might be organized otherwise. In this sense, prefiguration becomes not only a political tactic but also an artistic method, where the testing of new forms of value, authorship, and cooperation are lived and embodied. Through such practices, artists make tangible the provisional and yet vital negotiations of what collective life beyond inherited models could be.

Castells refers to prefiguration as "timeless time." It is an experience of time during a protest when the participants are free of the constraints of their routines, live in the moment in terms of their experience, and organize as if they were already living in their utopia.[141] There is no difference between the present and the future goals: the ideals become the norms ruling the protestors' present. This dislocated time is analogous to the temporal matrix of blockchain. The ex-ante regulatory framework is based on an agreed-upon value system that determines the experience of the present of the community through smart contracts that, in turn, also define their future interactions.

Barbara Cueto: Blockchain has gone through many waves, and we are now in the middle of the crypto-winter. Could distributed ledger technology still be saved?

Geert Lovink: The idea of decentralized financial infrastructures is something that still appeals to many. When we're talking about this being a tool for the redistribution of wealth, a lot of people say: "oh really?" Yeah, of course! At the moment crypto is only associated with corruption, Mafia practices, criminality and worst of all, with self-made billionaires, and with an enormous unprecedented form of the concentration of power and wealth. But does that mean that the original promise to use decentralized financial infrastructures for this redistribution is wrong? No, it doesn't. Blockchain is a poison, but it's also a cure. Future protest movements and countercultural practices will need its own infrastructure to sustain itself. Otherwise, people will just be lonely, they will be on their own, and they will be complete victims of the neoliberal order, which says that everything in the world is your problem because you failed. To oppose that, we need to create forms of togetherness.

Prefigurative tactics are value-loaded activities that provoke an affective union among the participants in a social movement. In my opinion, blockchains come to provide structures of belonging to the community. The precursory meshworking and the incipient commonality of the social movements in the early 2010s is the breeding ground that blockchain ecosystems bring to fruition. These systems carry the intentions and values born out of prefigurative dreams of the people in assemblies that never quite saw their hope crystallize, but whose essence still looks for their own space of autonomy.

CONCLUSION

To understand how artists find in blockchain a tool for their radical imagination, it was first necessary to examine how the technology operates and what its political implications might be. Any attempt to explore blockchain's emancipatory potential must begin by acknowledging its embeddedness within the very structures it sometimes seeks to resist. Blockchain is not outside capitalism; it is born from it and continues to operate through many of its logics. Yet it also opens a space to intervene in those logics, to reconfigure relationships of value, ownership, and governance from within. It becomes a site of struggle and experimentation, where the infrastructure of capital is bent toward collective and speculative ends. Artists in particular have shown how this double bind can be a source of creative force: adopting and repurposing the technology not as a solution, but as a provocation to imagine and enact alternatives.

De Angelis holds that "if we do not ground our critique of mainstream discourse on the problematisation of this law of value, then we will not be able to gain discursive, practice and political autonomy from the interests and value practices of capital."[142] To do so, chapter 1 of this book has explored the potentials of blockchain as a disruptive structure that could propose different notions of value, one that is noncapitalocentric. Rather than attempt to exhaustively describe blockchain's financial possibilities or provide a comprehensive political overview, the goal of chapter 1 was to examine the social potential of blockchain technology as the ground where artists can intervene and reconstruct to generate their own imaginaries.

Consequently, my analysis has focused on blockchain's capacity to reformulate social relations and readdress power structures in order to expose its potential to become an apparatus for social constructions of autonomy. Chapter 1 is an invitation to rethink blockchain as an organizational tool that can build pockets of resistance to empower communities in their quest for emancipation. In this way, we could start understanding how artists reappropriate and think through the very rigid technology to convey their shared values and goals. I do this because the technology is not going to code away all our problems. Blockchain needs to be understood politically in order to have the ability to redesign *socially*.

Each distinct configuration of a blockchain constructs its own social reality, not only because the use of the blockchain is based on a particular worldview, but also because this decentralized technology has the capacity to stage those specific versions. It can prefiguratively embody the political imaginary that was previously only aimed at. This is the productive milieu where artists working with blockchains queer the notion of value. This emancipatory capacity is plural, since the redistribution of the sensible is manifold. Blockchain, therefore, can be created and recreated, continually adapting its polymorphic composition to a particular worldview, desire, and value. Blockchain is a tool that can enact any type of project. Chapter 1 investigated the margins of economic discourses and practices at the outskirts of the political terrain. The goal is to think of the technology not as a capital venture, but instead as a social apparatus that could formulate value otherwise. Blockchain is not inherently revolutionary, but it can trigger revolution.

Digital decentralized ecosystems enhance criticality and raise the desire for autonomy, constituting radical forms of self-organization that carry prospects and attitudes that are introduced through a newfound sense of self-determination. Decentralization not only provides alternative forms of coordination, but it also brings about value in a community. This underlying relationship between decentralization and value becomes a fundamental notion to foster the desire for autonomy within the structure.

The subversive potential of blockchain is rooted in its plasticity, which permits the molding of new rules, institutions, social orders, politics, and economies. Blockchain not only disintermediates institutions, it also becomes the very institutions that it succeeds. Hayes argues that "due to the flexible, configurable, and open nature of blockchain code, they are indeed sandboxes for institution creation and experimentation."[143] Those new substitute blockchain institutions could overcome capitalist thought, liberating the notion of value from the subjugation of that hegemonic conceptualization. By queering it, as Gibson-Graham would say, value becomes plural and diverse.

Far away from productivity, scarcity, or property, value is ethical and communitarian—worth is allocated to what makes the *commonality of being*.[144] Blockchain can, in this way, compose a governance structure that could readdress immanent power dynamics in the group by providing visibility and assessing the relevance of the tasks that come to support the *making* of the community. As a result, this alternative techno-social configuration can spawn social formations that make visible often-forgotten tasks such as care labor, conflict management, social innovation, or social reproductions.[145]

This decentralized technology can organize these incipient ecosystems as autonomous, separate from the world of global finance, by programming social and economic relations in a peer-to-peer manner, thereby fostering social surplus. Consequently, blockchain technologies become hyperpolitical tools that can overcome the current sociopolitical stagnation due to distrust of our political systems. It does so by virtue of an alternative mode of organizing economic activity that is not based on the accumulation of capital. Artists take up these tools to reinvent institutions and foster communities that stand in contrast to the logic of the ones that host them, whether the museum, the gallery, or the residency. Artists use blockchain to imagine systems of fair payment, collective governance, and distributed agency, reshaping the conditions under which art is made, circulated, and valued. As a result, blockchains offer paths to emancipation thanks to the structural versatility of the technology's affordances, which provide a resilient framework to channel alternative worldviews. Blockchain can, therefore, channel the manifold compositions of different communities from a social movement, endowing them with a new hybrid space of possibility. By occupying the symbolic digital space, blockchain, appropriated by these communities, can meticulously adjust its governance to respond to the shared value systems and collective goals. Blockchain becomes a space of autonomy. And what would that look like? We will see in chapters 2 and 3 how artists reappropriate, reconstruct, and reinvent blockchain to shape and envision the proposals that create new social imaginaries.

2 POETICS OF BLOCKCHAIN

Metal paint tubes are simple packaging tools. They are both durable and lightweight enough to be carried around without being broken. Invented in 1841 by artist John Goffe Rand, this small innovation was one of the greatest transformations in painting a field where the previous technical revolution took place around the fifteenth century, when egg yolk was replaced by oil in binding pigment.[1] Before metal tubes, artists could only prepare a few colors per session according to whatever they were going to paint on that precise day. The new paint tubes eliminated time constraints. Paint became accessible, portable, and always fresh. And with metal tubes came another improvement: the color choice in pre-mixed paint grew exponentially. In the previous years, industrial chemist research discovered industrial pigments. Cobalt blue emerged in 1807; cadmium yellow in 1820; viridian in 1838; cerulean blue in 1860, to be followed by synthetic French ultramarine, zinc white, and cobalt violet. And let us not forget that pigments had remained unchanged since the Renaissance.

In 1839, shortly before metal paint tubes were conceived, Louis Daguerre and Henry Fox Talbot, independently of each other, invented photography. For centuries, Western art had been dominated by artists' focus on detailed realism. Photography changed our perspective of the world, our understanding of movement and the shape of composition. The camera replaced the painter as the producer of truth. Painting was freed to explore new forms of representation. Metal tubes with vibrant colors appeared just as painters were trying to push the boundaries of traditional painting. They could go outside and think beyond the limitations of the one-point perspective of the Renaissance. These radical changes caused a crisis. When the Impressionist artists began to paint *plein air*, and without the strict parameters set by centuries of trying to imitate nature, they were expelled from the same art exhibition circuit that they aimed to revolutionize. Their work was not selected to be included in the Paris Salon, the most prestigious art event at that time. News of a complaint by a group of artists, which included Gustave Courbet, Édouard Manet, and Camille Pissarro, made its way to Emperor Napoleon III. It resulted in Le Salon des Refusés of 1863: an exhibition held at the same time as the Paris Salon where the controversial artists could exhibit their work. Widely attended and even more criticized, this event marked a before and after in the history of art.

Art history is the study of the history and development of the visual arts. But art history is not only about the evolution of the artist's skills or the audience's tastes, it also goes hand in hand with technological evolution. Technology radically enhances, expands, and transforms the artist's capacity. Far from destroying art, as some might claim, technology makes possible what was previously impossible. Inevitably, with every innovation comes a new form of dissent.

Digital technologies such as text-to-image AI like Midjourney or Stable Diffusion, or large language models like ChatGPT, are disrupting the principles of what we have come to understand to be original, authentic, and true. Or are they? Perhaps, now more than ever, it is important to remind ourselves that these conversations are far from unique. These innovations are a call for a new model, which inevitably brings about a resistance, before the old one finally disappears. The evolution of art history is inextricably linked to technological innovation and, with it, rupture.

In chapter 2, I propose a survey exploring the lineage opened by the myriad encounters of art and technology, which have provided ongoing forms of experimentation that expand the limits of both fields, testing audience experiences and issues of museological practice, such as conservation, curation, and display. This chapter continues with an exploration of artistic practices using blockchain, analyzing its social potential. Therefore, I do not focus on all blockchain-related artworks, but only those that are interested in the technology in order to trigger social production and reproduction.

Chapter 2 strives to move beyond a description of medium specificity, understanding digital art as a form of critique attuned to the problems and concerns of a postdigital society. I intend to offer a different framework of analysis, situating the heirs of new media as a form of critique engaging with accelerated algorithmic futures and their postdigital communities. I consider the variety of artistic practices using blockchain, which means that I will not focus exclusively on DAOs or NFTs. My goal is to look across the board, considering artworks that think *through* the technology and engage with its affordances to generate new social imaginaries only possible because of the technology. As a result, this chapter strives to trace the outset of the artistic practices working with blockchains, elaborating a lineage that continues institutional critique and formulates a new version of socially engaged format that is grounded in the legacy of the avant-garde.

DIGITAL ART AS INSTITUTIONAL CRITIQUE

In 2012, art historian Claire Bishop started an essay in *Artforum* with the question: "What happened to digital art?"[2] In it, she describes how little digital practices overlap with the mainstream art world, although production of visual arts is profoundly influenced by digital means. In her view, the artistic practices of the moment were a reaction against the digital. She mentions the allure of analog films; socially engaged art as a response to the disembodiment of the digital; and "archival impulse" as a way to foster human interpretation rather than machinic reprocessing. "My point is that mainstream contemporary art simultaneously disavows and depends on the digital revolution, even—especially—when this art declines to speak overtly about the conditions of living in and through new media," she explains.

But 2012 feels like a lifetime ago, when the future looked bright, Obama was still president, and Twitter was a public agora. It is now clear what happened afterward. If digital art, or new media as it was referred to, was flying under the radar, now it is almost impossible to avoid. From AI products like ChatGPT, Stable Diffusion, and Midjourney, to game engines becoming ubiquitous tools for world-building, digital tools have never been more present in exhibitions, magazines, and public programs. The digital has become inseparable from our nowness.

In the twentieth century, the concept of art evolved to include new expressions, such as performances, installations, or artifacts from non-Western traditions. However, digital art and new media has always stayed in the margins of this ever-growing family of artistic practices. "New media" is a broad term that acts as an umbrella hosting any artworks produced, modified, or transmitted through any emerging technology. By its very nature, it challenges the limits that shape the structures of the art world: from conventional models of ownership and distribution, to participation and interaction. Although its status is no longer in question, I would argue that its analysis is not yet complete and is often involved only with aesthetics, which leaves out other productive sources of investigation.[3] Therefore, chapter 3 offers a different approach: one that inscribes digital art within the tradition of institutional critique, which is here understood as a method instead of a historical period.[4] Though they are often seen to have separate genealogies, new media art and institutional critique share distinctive features such as formal experimentation, participation, and collaboration. These characteristics call into question the authority of the institution as a system of valorization. Therefore, my examination aims at continuing the lineage of new media, including new digital practices, inserting them within the institutional critique canon.

Institutional critique is, as art historian Hal Foster asserts, "a crossing—of institutions of art and political economy, of representations of sexual identity and social life."[5] Following two consecutive waves, the term "institutional critique" evolved and tapped into different ways of addressing the institutional context, related to a shift in the understanding of space. In the first wave, during the 1960s and 1970s, space was conceptualized as a social construction. Philosopher Oliver Marchart considers space not as an unchanging, ever-existing arena where society has been built upon, but instead notes that "the specific structure of space was the result of social, economic and political process."[6] Institutional space was thus a rendering of the power structures of the art world and, consequently, its financial and political principles.

In an attempt to disrupt property circuits, the first wave's artists responded with dematerialization and conceptualization, putting new emphasis on processes and communication.[7] Performance art acquired the status of art. It became a form of criticism in itself, addressing the political and economic conditions of the physical location that hosted them: the art institution.[8] This first wave of dematerialization was thus a symptom and a reaction to the system, a way to subvert those structures, with Foster notoriously claiming that the institution had become a target and weapon.[9] However, despite artists' desire to problematize the institutional model, those same institutions quickly took over the movement itself. Art could not avoid the power of the market and the institutions of power, and could not escape its cycles of appropriation and speculation. The art market ended up assimilating and swallowing conceptual art.

Contemporaneous to this first wave, new media arose as a new form of artistic experimentation. It shared the same processual and dematerialized nature, although it was rooted on the outskirts of art circles, rendering different power structures. New media's critique was thus addressed to other hegemonic systems, which weren't necessarily related to the politics and economics of the art world, making this genre less susceptible to their co-option. The first incubators of new media art were defense-funded universities and industry research labs, where artists and engineers collaborated in pioneering investigations without a fixed ideology. For instance, cybernetic artist Max Bense was conducting media investigations with independence from the art world. Interestingly, his concept *Informationsästhetik*[10] substitutes the traditional idea of the artwork for a more all-encompassing, open-ended notion of "objects that are exposed to aesthetic judgement."[11] That is to say, the borders between scientific and artistic experimental uses of computers were not clear-cut. As media theorist Max Zeilinger clarifies, the "refusal of early experimental practitioners to choose between binary options ('Is this art or research?') was a commitment to developing truly new frameworks for, and approaches to, digital art-making and human-computer interaction."[12] Thus, as Johanna Drucker argues, the process of "technologising art and aestheticising technology were complementary impulses at the time."[13]

Already in the 1950s, Fluxus artists Nam June Paik and Wolf Vostell worked with televisions and started their dream of creating an artist-run TV broadcast, which would materialize years later. These works underlined processual and event-focused practices, whose eccentric nature facilitated a higher degree of autonomy from the art world, and the capacity to question the institution in a more immanent manner. Like conceptual art, these practices also tended toward dematerialized, processual, collaborative, and event-based practices. Of course, however, they were conditioned by the materials, the hardware, and the still-limited possibilities.[14] Inevitably, new media art has always been profoundly determined by the rich evolution in communication and technology, which came to be its investigative focus.

For art historian Alexander Alberro, these 1960s radical practices are related to the proliferation and velocity of new formats, types of consumption, and an increase in advertising, as well as swifter change in fashion and style cycles.[15] One can think of conceptual practices like the mail art of the New York Correspondence School or the Xerox Book of Seth Siegelaub. These projects surged as a reaction to this acceleration, dissipating the relevance of sole authorship, and dematerializing practice to circumvent the market. Correspondingly, Fluxus's formal experimentations brought to the fore the figure of the audience and encouraged new ways of involvement, where instructions or scores set in motion audience participation. For example, Dick Higgins's *Intermedia Object #1* (1966) materialized in performable scores that were used in a Happening. These Fluxus works highlighted three issues: first, the necessity of an engagement with an audience, which became more active in the reception and the making of the artwork; second, they underlined the immaterial nature of the artwork; and third, they paid attention to the aesthetic potential of everyday life, surpassing the museum as the only platform for artistic experiences.[16]

A layer of code and a set of instructions is what connects Dada and Fluxus experiments with formal variations and the conceptual pieces by Duchamp, John Cage, and Sol LeWitt. All these practices are based on an execution of rules.[17] If we think of NFTs, this idea becomes even clearer, as these artworks are contracts or certificates, again another layer of code or instructions, that are stored in a blockchain, pointing toward a jpg or gif, which is then stored somewhere else. What one owns is a certificate, not an image. Ultimately, both new media practitioners of the avant grade and conceptual artists used similar types of formal experimentation to engage with the institutional structures that support them. However, new media artists managed to avoid, more or less successfully, the commodification of their work by the market until recently and by the rise of NFTs as objects of desire. This lack of commercial desirability had a collateral effect too: the market was not their source of valorization.

In the 1980s, the understanding of space was again revised and reinterpreted. Whereas the first wave of institutional critique questioned the authoritarian role of the cultural institution, the artists of the second wave switched their attention to the politics of representation within such institutions. Whereas the first wave of institutional critique questioned the authoritarian role of the cultural institution, the artists of the second wave switched their attention to the politics of representation within such institutions. These practices happened within the museum's borders, not engaging with its specifics, as did the preceding generation, but utilizing it as a proxy for all institutions, which came to represent the hierarchies of power.

The coetaneous new media art responded to the changed notion of space differently, having in mind the specific characteristics of its medium, and the particular political context of the structures that support it. These artists were more aware and responsive to technological innovations as well as to developments in the history of technology and media sciences. For instance, *Many Voices, One World: Towards a New, More Just, and More Efficient World Information and Communication Order*, known as "the MacBride Report," published in 1980 by UNESCO, is one of the first comprehensive studies on the connection between media and power. The report delved into how disparate access to communications affects the economic and political development of nations, their inhabitants, and individuals.[18] Media artists reacted to these kinds of theoretical advances by putting the spotlight on world media infrastructures and their influence on society. The critical engagement of new media art was rerouted toward the techno-cultural complex, instead of focusing on representation within fine art institutions and acting within its confines. But things changed with digital art, opening up a new set of possibilities with more nuanced critique.

Nettime mailing list was one of the main vectors of distribution of net art in the 1990s, and it brought together artists, theorists, media activists, and programmers. It empowered immanent critique of an internet that was still in its infancy, investigating its techno-scientific structures while they were still developing. This critique via Nettime was embedded in the network itself, using the same tools and languages with the goal of influencing and shaping future developments. For art historian Brian Holmes, this format reveals a double movement with the two waves of institutional critique overlapping in the same new media practices. One is an inward movement that addresses the particularities of the medium from within; the other looks outward, seeking change outside the realm of action, by addressing the power structures at large.

Digital art continues the lineage of new media and enhances the project of critique in a new manner. It does so because it can circumvent the art system of valorization and commodification, which it doesn't need for either production or presentation.[19] Digital art, therefore, holds a novel sense of agency that translates into a more systematic critique of the institutions of power, and is far-reaching in its approach. From research visualizations to interactive installations, digital artworks are symptoms of the techno-political context, as well as agents against it.[20] They continue to deepen the project of institutional critique and generate new formats that are attuned to the current forms of algorithmic oppression and control, stretching out of the institution itself. For example, the multidisciplinary group Forensic Architecture uses architectural techniques and new technologies to investigate cases of state violence and human rights violations around the world. Their polymorphic investigations are presented in museums, international courtrooms, parliamentary inquiries, and United Nations (UN) assemblies, as well as in citizens' tribunals and truth commissions. These projects are not considered *necessarily* art. They move between disciplines and act across institutions.

One of the obvious repercussions of COVID-19 for the art world was the burgeoning of online events ranging from digital exhibitions, and numerous online assemblies and conferences, to multiple online residency experiments. Although these curatorial approaches are gaining momentum, there are few that manage to successfully provide the right environment for the artworks and to stimulate audience engagement. These curatorial projects are conceived as if they were experiences in the physical realm, but they use digital tools as the most literal form of translation: a conference becomes a digital meeting (via a video platform) or a physical exhibition is rendered as a 3D interactive model (e.g., Google Maps). Using the same curatorial onsite strategies tends to go awry because they cannot provide the modes of engagement that can guarantee the proper unraveling of the artwork. Digital art challenges the very models that used to shape the traditional art institution presentation, which raises the question of its function in terms of display, mediation, and reproduction.

Digital artworks resist traditional and physical models as they frequently rely on code and reproductive data, which challenges issues of ownership, copyright, and branding.[21] On a technical level, these artworks need continuous upkeep and appropriate equipment. And that is why I think the inclusion of digital art in the museological context has been so slow—because it falls between practices, curatorial models, and forms of collaboration.

The materiality (or the lack thereof) is determined by digital art's process-oriented nature, which strives for collaboration. Furthermore, there is a subtle process of co-creation between nonhumans and humans that affects traditional notions of authorship and authenticity.[22] Thus, the role of artists evolves, as they frequently perform the role of facilitator, since they often work through collaborative networks of likeminded artists, programmers, researchers, curators, engineers, or scientists.[23] The raison d'être of this collaboration is political engagement, which drives artists together to further their research beyond the limits of an artistic or academic discipline.[24]

The critique coming from digital media expands across realms and calls for a much more fundamental inquiry into the institutions at large. By using formal experimentation and multidisciplinary and translocal collaboration, digital artists raise awareness in diverse audiences and provide new forms of interaction that exceed museological rationale. Practitioners of digital art aim at laying bare the structures of power to reveal this new reality, where digital and physical are on a continuum.

In this enlarged terrain of struggle, these practitioners go through and within the institutions to provide a nuanced and new understanding of institutional critique using a type of analysis that surpasses the art world and a type of engagement that reaches beyond museum goers. The art institution's traditional form and function is thus called into question, as neither its shape nor its function fulfills the necessities of these new types of experimentation with new technologies. Digital art is not an adaptation; it is native and speaks a critical digital vernacular. Inevitably, this represents a crisis, one that asks for the old model to slowly die, so that the new one might rise quickly.

SOCIALLY ENGAGED DIGITAL ART

As a ramification of the social turn,[25] new political, activist, and participatory practices emerged in the 1990s and crystallized in what is called socially engaged art. These terms are used to refer to a broad type of art projects that focus on participation and engagement with specific communities to achieve change on a local scale.[26] Like institutional critique, socially engaged art is committed to commentary on structures of power, but is ultimately concerned with and reacts against the effects of late capitalism.[27] As with institutional critique, digital art is a medium that has not been included within socially engaged art, although it shares many of its characteristics. Let's analyze tactical media, one of the canonical projects of digital art in the early 1990s.

Barbara Cueto: How would you describe tactical media?

Geert Lovink: Tactical media is always operating within the realm of social media and to wider social-political demands and practices, and has an agenda to intervene. Tactical media is grounded in the situation: in the event, in the location, in the local politics, and in the reality of the place. You can do graffiti, you can do something with multimedia, blockchain, a website, a blog, social networking or XYZ. The tactical aspect of it is really that you decide for each situation a particular way of intervention and a specific medium. In the 1990s, almost naturally we went to multimedia and the internet. In the Amsterdam context, it was about cables, videos, and television, exhibitions, graffiti, and pirate radio. Not necessarily performances like the Yes Men. But a lot of people ultimately associate the term [tactical media] with them, and I'm proud of that. There's a lot of inspiration people still take out of that.

In the 1990s the nascent internet provided a new communication channel that contemporary anti-globalization movements rapidly took over to create a new form of protest.[28] Tactical media reacted to the sweeping effects of neoliberalism by appropriating cheap, readily available technologies for engendering political resistance in socially disenfranchised populations.[29] This appropriation generated a new form of engagement with audiences and power structures alike, just like the coetaneous critical practices. Tactical media not only entailed a new form of activism with new skill sets and wide-ranging actions, but also encouraged the integration of politics, aesthetics, and technology, which is a key legacy of this movement.[30]

Barbara Cueto: What would then be, if any, the next embodiment of that interventionism or tactical media?

Gregory Sholette: The early internet phenomena promised fundamental social change. People like Lawrence Lessig were claiming that people are going to have direct access to democratic institutions using these digital networks, and that could move towards direct democracy.[31] And therefore, you're gonna have this complete toppling of old, creaky bureaucratic governmental structures. It is important to remember that the Cold War and socialism just had ended, and everything was very centralized at that time. This new technology allowed people to communicate across the world, which seemed like a recipe for the flowering of democracy. But we know it comes to a very bitter end. Especially after 9/11, because before there was a grey zone. People like Ricardo Dominguez could do like a virtual sit-in the government of Mexico to protest what was happening in Chiapas with the Zapatistas, by flooding their internet site.[32] And now it's completely illegal. 9/11 accelerated clamping down on the internet and its potential for good and for bad. Tactical media had its moment in that bright, early part of the internet utopia, and then it crashed along with what happened with the internet. And I don't think it's going to be revived at this point.

The Tactical Media Manifesto[33] spawns a reflection that addresses the power of the digital commons around the 2000s,[34] highlighting them "as a space for sharing, learning, and collaborative culture in general" and thus forgoing the more combative contours of virtual protest.[35] This adjustment to tactical media's endeavor came as a response to the intensive lobbying of the tech industry to strengthen policies around copyright protection in the digital realm. This implicitly changed tactical media's time-scope from short-term thinking and immediate action to a long-term commitment to establishing sustainable, free, and accessible alternatives. By developing, using, and promoting free and open source software (FOSS), tactical media intended to offer a substitute to the draconian copyright laws. These digital practices are inevitably grounded in the second wave of institutional critique, denouncing the institutions of power from within. The development of a community is also fundamental as a way of acting in epistemic swarms to fight against control and revealing the oppression of the techno-political complex.

In this framework, the notion of community acquires a new meaning. It makes visible the importance of the being-with, which Gibson-Graham assure us is the cornerstone of "the counter-hegemonic project of 'differently politicising' the economy."[36] Far from relational aesthetics, the notion of communal experiences denotes a political aspiration. It does so because it becomes a way to foster social surplus to trigger social change and counteract individualizing neoliberal forces, the passivity of the audience, and the disempowerment of nonauthors.[37]

The output of any socially engaged project is kinship relations, and the development of collaborating formats. Naturally, this transformation is the result of the progressive dematerialization and formal experimentation that started with the first wave of institutional critique and the coetaneous new media art. They are immaterial practices that can only be experienced first-hand and require long-term commitment. This also alters the nature of the author. While it had previously required a figure as the facilitator of an experience, for instance Fluxus scores or LeWitt's instructions, now, the author becomes a collaborator. In turn, the role of the audience shifts: it turns into a co-producer of a collective experience. The goal of these projects is, therefore, to achieve a certain group dynamic, a social situation, a change of energy, a raised consciousness.[38] Socially engaged art procures, consequently, a site of collective action that reverberates with Gibson-Graham's social surplus notion. To these economic geographers, these are sites where new economic becomings take place, "sites where ethical decisions can be made, power can be negotiated and transformations forged."[39] Critical practices act similarly, which endows them with more than a critical voice, as they also have an empowering agency.

Socially engaged art also challenged two fundamental concepts traditionally linked to art appreciation that are radically called into question: aesthetics and criticism. They repudiate aesthetics, as they were considered, according to Bishop, "merely visual and (at worst) an elitist's realm of unbridled seduction complicit with spectacle."[40] The halt on authorship also exempts these practices of art criticism, since they are assessed only in terms of a set of ethical precepts.[41] In this context, art institutions are not at the center of this artistic experience, but are instead relegated to a secondary position, as socially engaged art doesn't necessarily make use of the institutional context to succeed.

Socially engaged practices go a step further, "by establishing ersatz institutions, or mock institutions, with intentionally unstable public identities . . . they [express] their goal of establishing an entirely autonomous political cultural sphere."[42] For example, the Silent University by Ahmet Ögut "is an autonomous knowledge exchange platform by and for refugees, asylum seekers and migrants. It is led by a group of lecturers, consultants and research fellows and is presented using the format of an academic program."[43] And INLAND by Fernando García-Dory is "an arts collective, dedicated to agricultural, social, and cultural production, and a collaborative agency," "a para-institution, working together, against and beyond existing institutions."[44] Digital socially engaged art functions similarly. They also build their own para-infrastructures to develop their activist projects, which move seamlessly between online and offline sites. Later in this chapter, I will explain this in relation to blockchain, and how a DAO culminates this process.

Barbara Cueto: How can we measure success in the art world? What are the units of that measuring tape?

Gregory Sholette: It's complicated, because we don't usually go into a museum and look at a painting and say, does it work? Is it successful in the same way as a political campaign, which for example aimed at getting rid of an incinerator that's polluting the neighborhood? If we got rid of it, the campaign was successful social engagement. We don't usually ask that question, though, of an artwork. And that begins to become problematic when artworks take on the same minds and goals as social activists. Stephen Wright uses a very nice formulation, saying that art scales itself up to the scale of reality.[45] You get to that point where you really couldn't slide a piece of the thinnest paper between what is real world activism and an artwork. They're not separable.

You have something like the artistic project *Conflict Kitchen*, where these two artists associated with the University of Pittsburgh created a fast-food restaurant with cuisines from places that were in conflict with the United States, changing the cuisine every few months.[46] They would also talk about the history of the country and the conflict. What interested me about it was it seemed to fit with my idea of Dark Matter as getting brighter, with these peripheral practices suddenly becoming much more visible. It was getting amazingly great reviews on Yelp by just people who would go there to get a sandwich. They managed to have a staff of twenty. Even though they were subsidized by the university, they probably could have just run it as a business. But later, the employees tried unionizing because they wanted to get a minimum wage of $15 per hour. The people behind the project said yes, but that led to the demise of the project, they don't exist any longer. When something turns into a real-world thing, it then has to face the real world.

Getting back to the question of measuring success. As a . . . pedagogical project [*Conflict Kitchen*] didn't really do well. It got itself shut down. But as a restaurant project, it worked really well, it was successful to the point where it could have become autonomous. So, we are in limbo. We don't have any terminology, or any real language to describe what it was artistically. The ideas of relational

> aesthetics or participatory art could probably apply . . . here. But none of that feels really like it's getting to the heart of the problem.

Fundamentally, the intention of social, participatory practices is to activate the audience members "to emancipate them from the state of alienation induced by the dominant ideological order—be this consumer capitalism, totalitarian socialism, or military dictatorship."[47] As a result, these polymorphic socially engaged processes have very diverse outcomes but share political resolution, often under the imaginary of the commons, as happened with tactical media. The practice of making digital art has clear advantages, such as digital art's inherent immateriality, the adaptability of its potential physical translations, and wide online reach and engagement. As we know, digital artists work directly with code, meaning that the outcome of their work could be an app or a website, for example. However, it is often the case that these digital native artworks are curated in traditional physical exhibitions. For them, these projects are translated into an installation or a video. Not being the primary medium of the artwork makes them potentially changeable and adaptable to the circumstances of the exhibition. If we think again about the Forensic Architecture projects, they take different forms adjusted to the exhibition venue. To better understand how all these characteristics play out in digital practices, I will now turn to a case study of *HyperReadings*, a digital and decentralized art project that generates a collective and nonhierarchical process of sharing and learning.

HyperReadings

HyperReadings is an artistic project by Sean Dockray, Benjamin Forster, and Julia Bavyka that was presented as part of *This site is under Revolution*, an exhibition that I curated as a Strategic

Project during the 6th Moscow International Biennale for Young Art at the Moscow Museum of Modern Art (MMOMA) in the summer of 2018. The project is a digitally distributed archival infrastructure for writing, sharing, navigating, and adapting reading lists. As such, it embodies a socially engaged practice, which uses the digital as a milieu to empower the user to share and enable a collective process of knowledge production and distribution. At MMOMA, it took the shape of open-source software, a reading group, an installation, and a series of workshops. As open-source software, *HyperReadings* was developed and maintained by Sean Dockray and Benjamin Forster, while Julia Bavyka joined this informal and porous collaboration, contributing to the physical manifestation and communication of this largely intangible infrastructure. For the biennale, MMOMA became a node in the distributed infrastructure, a physical and digital host of *HyperReadings*.

HyperReadings provided computational resources in support of the broader P2P network, and physical space for collective sharing, reading, writing, and ultimately learning together. As Forster put it, "Sharing what we read, what we want to read, and what we think other people should read becomes a form of peer-to-peer education, the propagation of informal and personal canons."[48] In this way, *HyperReadings* offered a physical and virtual space of co-learning that employed the readings lists, which became aesthetic objects to both organize and produce knowledge. Formally, *HyperReadings* involved software that creates and adapts reading lists, and an installation in which a series of discursive events took place. The project was activated through its audience, whose members are co-producers of a collective experience through a digital app or workshops or both.

Reading lists serve as tools for contesting established patterns in public thinking, but also, importantly, for publicly making sense of our current times. In this context, *HyperReadings* became a subtle way to open a safe space in Moscow, where an audience could potentially express and share members' opinions. A key example to help understand the relevance of reading lists today is the syllabus "Women and Gender Nonconforming People Writing about Tech," published in September 2017. The syllabus was a response to the compilation by the *Los Angeles Review of Books* titled "The Digital Revolution: Debating the Promise and Perils of the Internet and Algorithmic Lives in the Last Years of the Obama Administration,"[49] which had only one contribution (a chapter in an edited collection) written by a woman. This collaboratively written online list was aimed at exposing lack of diversity and is composed of books by more than three hundred women and gender-nonconforming scholars, researchers, activists, writers, and speakers.

These reading lists were a format that triggered the project as a whole, offering a way to engage with local communities to share knowledge and open up conversation. The intention was to establish a tacit form of resistance coming both from the audience and the technology. In the case of *HyperReadings*, the audience was exchanging sources and opening up to new knowledge (potentially political). Moreover, using a decentralized protocol was both political and practical. As a decentralized infrastructure, an online reading list couldn't be tampered with or censored. Furthermore, due to its open-source nature, it embodied a commons-based economy, giving both programmers and end-users control over the software and, subsequently, over their devices.

Like socially engaged art, the reading list model was conceived as a response to neoliberal policies, in particular to the collateral damage occasioned by knowledge enclosure.[50] In particular, the artists behind *HyperReadings* had in mind the availability of digital libraries and advocated for the survival of small archives and individual collections. Also, like critical art practices, the project focused on commoning strategies, which promoted self-organization, social inclusion, and egalitarian participation. In them, care is taken to balance power among participants and to broaden the areas of people's lives that are based on democratic self-management.[51] Digital commoning becomes the way to challenge capitalocentric economic systems. By using Free/Libre software, the artists were able to engage with a community united by their shared project of resistance.

HyperReadings is built upon Dat Protocol, like BitTorrent, for instance. Dat is a peer-to-peer protocol for syncing folders of data, which implies that it distributes libraries across computers. Dat Library sustains *HyperReadings*, and its goal is to support scientific knowledge in a decentralized manner to secure accessibility. The project implements reading lists or a structured set of pointers (a list, a syllabus, a bibliography, etc.) into one or more libraries. *HyperReadings* is an open-source code, always available and reproducible, which empowers the audience in the process of co-creation. As both Lucy Lippard and Boris Groys acknowledge, activist art takes action, and likewise, *HyperReadings* offers a real alternative education, using a P2P education model.[52] And thus becomes another example of a Mock-Institution that defined the socially engaged practices.

Moreover, the technology manages to find a way to surpasses stringent neoliberal copyright laws, facilitating an infrastructure that can disseminate texts freely, acting as the ground for a P2P learning environment. When it was installed at MMOMA, *HyperReadings* also became a physical structure in the form of a reading room containing bulletin boards, printers, computers, and seats. This analog version used the computers and printers to have the lists in situ, the pin boards became the online dashboard, and the furniture worked as infrastructure to support the discursive events.

The intention was for the audience to become involved in any way they wanted, denoting the importance of the being-with that Gibson-Graham understand as the keystone to formulating a counter-hegemonic project of resistance. Accordingly, Forster said, "The infrastructure accommodates the needs and desires of new users/audiences/communities and allows them to enter and contort the technology to their uses. It is infinitely hospitable."[53] Forster also recalled librarian and mathematician S. R. Ranganathan's last "Law of Library Science," which referred to the library as a living organism.[54] Reading lists offered a playful and productive context that could be infinitely adapted and reworked. In this way, *HyperReadings* connects the latter with the desire to forge a community of agents and it develops a sense of kinship among all participating: audience members, programmers, reading group contributors, and leaders. This system of cooperation replicated the code and generated a decentralized, nonhierarchical approach, where all the nodes could participate as equals in this mode of informal education. The digital project aroused a strong sense of community thanks to the transversal collaborations, openness toward participation, and broad thematic approach.

HyperReadings embodied the intentions of socially engaged art. Formally, it emphasized the process over obtaining a clear outcome, and its purpose was to generate a community that could share knowledge in a commons-based structure. However, a digital project has specific differences from and productive advantages over traditional socially engaged projects, which makes a digital undertaking responsive to the needs of today's society. Accordingly, *HyperReadings* has a more complex structure that moves across realms to create a translocal community of participants. It also generates a resilient, decentralized infrastructure to share digital commons opposing any possible commercialization. The digital project's workings also reverberate with a community economy, as described by Gibson-Graham. This is because *HyperReadings* was conceived as a system ruled by nonmarket values, which generated a collective experience of cooperation that resisted the logic of capitalism.

Conceptually, the sessions of *HyperReadings* mimicked the spirit of the commons, and offered a structure as both a virtual and physical environment where one could share knowledge. It overcame the digital divide and, with it, surpassed the medium specificity that characterized new media practice. The project was also being maintained and continually recreated by its users/producers, who adapted the infrastructure to their requirements and wishes. In this way, the project became a living entity, which survived through its community, as it produced something of collective value *with* the public, rather than *for* them.

NAVIGATING THE INTERSECTION OF SOCIALLY ENGAGED ART AND INSTITUTIONAL CRITIQUE

In 2021, Beeple sold an NFT at Christie's for $69,346,250 USD.[55] This event marked a change of paradigm: digital art was not only sellable, but also desirable. Suddenly, blockchain narratives moved from obscure techno-economic circles to the mainstream art market. Prices skyrocketed. Galleries jumped into the frenzy. And then, inflation arrived and, with it, the crypto-winter. But although investments are not volatile, conversations simmered and projects became more nuanced. We can now find many different types of projects using distributed ledger technology beyond NFTs with a jpg on them. In chapter 2, I will focus on the various artworks that think *through* the technology to propose counter-hegemonic projects. They do not necessarily utilize the technology to create commodifiable outputs, like the classic NFTs fever we saw before.[56] Rather, their works draw on the technology as a tool for radical imagination, which removes the emphasis from the final work and highlights the ongoing artistic process and the relevance of the collaborative making. These practices, as opposed to crypto assets, convey speculative moments of world-building, empowering multilocal and multidisciplinary communities and generating new systems of cooperation. At the same time, they remain immersed in the logic of capitalism, as the technology itself is a product of it. This tension is not ignored but becomes part of the work, forming the very terrain that artists navigate and push against in their effort to construct alternatives. As a result, they expand the notion of institutional critique and socially engaged art by providing a much more exhaustive critique and experiment with new collaboration systems. Critical Blockchain Art helps envision the potential of blockchain beyond hyperfinancialization. But first, I will explain how these practices situate themselves in the art history canon.

Liquid Dependencies is a game created by designer Yin Aiwen. The goal of this game is to build a commons-oriented society based on mutual aid values through long-term relationships, as a response to the challenges of a deeply ingrained traditional, atomized, and patriarchal care relationship. The game is based on the blockchain decentralized app (dApp) known as ReUnion Network, which generates long-term P2P care contracts and relationship-driven cryptocurrencies. The intention of this dApp is to help people create bottom-up social organizations as their everyday and long-term safety net. The game uses live-action role-playing (LARP) as a methodology and, in this way, it simulates daily life *as if* the ReUnion Network will be functioning and players' everyday experiences will be determined not by cycles of money extraction, but rather with the focus on fostering values such as care and solidarity. Using cards and exchanging tokens, the game's participants experience changing conditions in their lives and, based on these circumstances, they make different decisions. What would happen if money were not a deciding factor in your decision-making process? Would you then get out of your way to help anyone? Would you behave differently with your family? Would you still go to work? What type of relationships would you pursue in a money-free society? In *Liquid Dependencies*, status is related to the process of weaving a safety net made of mutual support. In Yin's micro-utopia, tokens represent care between participants, not the market to establish factors of exchange. Through this gesture, she is able to queer economic languages and generates a lexicon of economic diversity anticipated by J. K. Gibson-Graham.

This project and many others, such as Dayra, discussed previously, are *written* in critical digital vernacular. They go a step further in their desire for emancipation by providing an independent, resilient, and adaptable digital structure to work within a community united by shared values and political awareness. As artistic experimentations they achieve what Gregory Sholette calls "critical autonomy," a self-validating mode of cultural production and distribution.[57] These art projects cannot be "unambiguously defined as art,"[58] and are created as a joint effort between multidisciplinary players in cooperative systems that evoke P2P collaboration. Like any other digital art form, they are both a symptom of and an agent against the techno-political context, responsive to a changed communication environment and technological development, and the repoliticization of the mediascape. These artworks, like new media art before them, are a reaction to the evolution of digital technologies and prompt a different type of inquiry. In this case, it is one that critically engages with the problems of our time by conjuring alternatives to shape new social imaginaries.

Due to their formal experimentation, participation, and collaboration, these artworks call into question the authority of the institution as a system of valorization through an analysis that surpasses the art world and a type of engagement that reaches beyond museum goers. The technology critically engages with the traditional hegemonic practices that position the market at the center of postdigital society, and they propose and experiment with potential alternatives to subvert those orders. For instance, Yin Aiwen suggests a society based on kin relations instead of money exchange. Utilizing tokens, these artistic projects can accordingly program and adapt their social and economic relations, which recasts blockchain into a situated technology[59] and, reciprocally, transforms the projects into a new form of socially engaged work. If the output of socially engaged art is a kinship relation, in blockchain, one finds kin tokens providing a "structure of belonging," an idea that I will later explain in detail.

Artists working with blockchains problematize the reproduction of the symbolic order of neoliberalism in the postdigital realm and create new forms of engagement that overcome the borders between the physical and the virtual, generating a community of like-minded collaborators with the same political outlook. For example, the art collective Black Swan intends to disrupt the art world economy by making artists the key holders, and enabling more solidarity between other interdependent artworks. They developed Cygnet, a decision-making application for artistic communes. It uses quadratic voting to decide to which artistic project it should allocate resources to produce it. A proposal is first submitted by the members of the artistic community, and token holders allocate their votes depending on their preference. Artists and creatives become the source of validation, not the market or institutions. The intention is to capture the value produced by artists and creative processes, and turn it into a sustainable economic process for artists.

Although the critique of the system of valorization and their transdisciplinary reach are the most common features of many of these projects, one can also observe an underlying form of criticism engaging with the precarious system of institutional funding. These projects fall between the cracks of traditional support mechanisms for arts or technology, either too techie for the art world, or too artful for the cryptosphere. Nevertheless, they are powerful gestures of worldling, as they imagine suitable economies adapted to their shared goals and values. "Beyond Cultures of Ownership: Emerging Strategies for Interdependence" was a 2023 conference organized by Serpentine Galleries in London and the think tank RadicalxChange.[60] Participants discussed the potential of using art and culture to rethink ownership models, as they "have always been instrumental in shaping narratives and norms, both in support of and in rejection of power."[61] Research projects like this, at the intersection of technologies, economy, and art, come to represent a renewed interest in art and its world-building capacity and its ability to redefine social imaginaries. They position art as a "relational structure rather than a form of capital—a complex of mutual obligations, rather than a fixed asset," whereby one can "unlearn our habits of approaching the world through a speculative lens and develop systems that emphasise interdependence through responsibility."[62]

Projects like the Sphere compose a comprehensive proposal to build sustainable, community-driven funding ecology for performing artists. Their manifesto states, "In order to reshape the economic game space toward commons-oriented purposes, we need techno-social devices and infrastructures that operate at the protocol level, digital governance tooling allowing for coordination at scale."[63] Using a DAO, this network of radical theorists, artists, and technologists are united through decentralized governance, resource allocation, and NFT-based co-ownership. The Sphere has developed different tools and working mechanisms to activate their world building. The Karmic Funding Cycle allows one to collect live art through

NFTs. It uses the Karmic Engine as a consensus-building tool (built upon Cygnet by Black Swan) and the Karmetplace as a marketplace. The Anarchiving Game makes it possible to mint, share, and collect fragments of the creative process. The Sphere Pavilion is a VR gallery displaying the artworks funded by the Karmic Funding Cycle. These initiatives take shelter under the umbrella concept Proof-of-Celebration, accomplishing the Sphere's goal of creating a broad mechanism to support live artists by reexamining traditional intellectual property frameworks.

Projects like these exemplify how artists critically engaging with blockchains continue the project of critique initiated with new media art, in which both waves of institutional critique overlap and create a new structure of collaboration that expands the potential of circuits where socially engaged art is hosted. The first wave looked inward and addressed the particularities of the medium from within, like Cygnet, whereby Black Swan implicitly call into question the authority, gatekeeping, and funding strategies of the traditional art world. In turn, the second wave looks outward, and tries to operate outside the realm of action, addressing the power structures at large. Black Swan's goal is to propose a system that prioritizes their community, and to advance a social imaginary determined by solidarity and care among peers. If we compare it to socially engaged practices, the output of projects like Cygnet or the Sphere's Proof-of-Celebration is not primordial: the process of collaboration between agents is of foremost importance. This approach reverberates with the goals of socially engaged art, which stimulate cooperation to counterbalance the individualizing neoliberal impetus.[64]

It is their critical autonomy that enables these artists to propose alternatives to circumvent algorithmic control, political fragmentation, and increasing hyperfinancialization. And, as a result, those who critically engage with distributed ledger technology not only are committed to institutional critique and social practice, but also are providing an answer and elaborating a radical proposal. I called these projects Critical Blockchain Art, which I will explain in more detail in chapter 3. But first I will continue on this winding road through art history.

THE LEGACY OF THE AVANT-GARDE

Distributed ledger technology does not exist in a vacuum. Neither do the artistic practices that work with blockchains. However, because of its relatively recent underlying technology and the general misrepresentation of digital practices in museological contexts, Critical Blockchain Art has almost always escaped from any art historical analysis. After trying to locate its roots in the practices of institutional critique and socially engaged art, I find myself wanting to position Critical Blockchain Art within a chronological, traditional, probably too Western, and likely incomplete art history. And in this way, I want to justify that these artworks, although often dismissed as such, have become heirs to the same desires for rupture, and hold the same utopian hopes that characterized the avant-garde movement many years ago. Or, at the very least, these works present a prefigurative manifestation of the same desires and hopes.

"We are the new people of a new life" proclaimed the Russian Cubo-Futurist manifesto in 1912.[65] These utopian statements were often present in manifestos or programmatic texts of the avant-garde. However, unlike earlier utopian forms—for example, Thomas More's *Utopia*[66]—the avant-garde wasn't based on progress and continuity, but on a clear rupture with the past. The future becomes, as art historians David Ayers and Benedikt Hjartarson argue, an open site for utopian projects abandoning its neutrality as an empty space for the unfolding of time.[67] Historian Reinhart Koselleck locates this shift in the eighteenth century, as histories no longer "take place in time, but through time."[68] In the political arena, this transformation leads to new revolutionary or totalitarian states, but in the aesthetic realm, the future and its utopian outlook envisioned a new world with a new social order that was profoundly indebted to the aesthetic imagination, with artists considered visionaries.[69]

Critical Blockchain Art has inadvertently inherited many features that have come to characterize the traditional avant-garde: it is praxis-oriented, focuses on collectivity to overcome capitalism, and is tinted with the hope of utopia. Furthermore, its subversive spirit and talent for defiance is similar to the critical power of the historical avant-garde. As art historian Grant Kester states, the avant-garde's "task is to transgress existing categories of thought, action, and creativity, to constantly challenge fixed boundaries and identities."[70] Analogously, art critically engaging with blockchains seeks to exercise new social paradigms with postcapitalist points of identification that test conventions within art, technology, and society alike. The notion of value comes up again with dual personality, presenting both rupture and novelty, along with resistance and hope. Despite the failed liberatory aims of past artistic and political vanguards, perhaps blockchain's liberation of value in the present is rekindling aspirations for a new "poetry of revolution," as philosopher Martin Puchner would say.[71]

The still-experimental nature of blockchain endows the art forms using this technology with an undeniable agency in its future development, moving away from speculation and influencing new proposals in the real world, while also questioning previous ones. These aesthetic experimentations represent futures that have not yet been co-opted by technological monopolies, and they help to envision new emancipatory strategies and push boundaries toward those futures. This lingering utopian sentiment accompanies many projects

in blockchain, as it did for the avant-garde. "Utopia as a form is not the representation of radical alternatives; it is simply the imperative to imagine them," asserts Fredric Jameson.[72] Utopia is, therefore, a method, which a multitude of artistic proposals put to work to depict new futures.

Barbara Cueto: The idea of the institution as a system of valorization comes up again and, with it, how artists had created mechanisms and practices to avoid it, like with the first wave of institutional critique, socially engaged practices, or new media. In the case of the artistic projects working with blockchains, they can also get validation through the tech sphere. Could these projects be relevant both in the art world and in the real world? Is it even possible to aim for both?

Gregory Sholette: The choice is: institution versus *not* institution. We have to acknowledge that you really don't escape institutionality as long as you're within the discourse of art practice. Even when I talk about Dark Matter, which [are the artists] that exist on the periphery, with seemingly invisible form. But nevertheless, the art world depends upon this idea of its periphery: Dark Matter is at the very center of the art world to do all the work. [This is] like MFA students putting up the walls for an exhibition of a famous artist, or working in some famous person's studio as an assistant.

The people who purposely try to escape institutionality by creating their own institutions are fulfilling the same project: banding together, collaborating, creating social structures that exist in the art world. This is the idea of a Mock-Institution. If there is success, they actually get visibility because they've created an entire fake persona. Digital tools made it so easy. One can make a logo and a website instead of relying on word-of-mouth.

You're really trying to reinvent the institution in [such] a way that you can actually still love it. We cry when the

> Museum of Modern Art or the Whitney does something really horrible, because we think of it as our world. There's just [as] much work in creating a fake institution as in making a real institution. You might as well have a real institution, or stop pretending, right? Maybe that's one answer. Whenever one tries to do anything, even with the smallest collective, [it] is a huge amount of work. And then you have to decide, well, how do we make decisions? Oh, that means we have to have some kind of voting mechanism. You're basically reinventing the institution from the inside out.

The avant-garde's driving force was the construction of a new society, culture, and humanity through aesthetic experiments and investigations.[73] The utopianism of these projects was driven by a praxis-oriented approach, as also happens in the case of Critical Blockchain Art. For example, the art collective Black Swan wanting to outdo the valorization process coming from the art institution; or Dayra hoping to create an exchange system without money. Therefore, these projects operate comparably to a Mock-Institution[74] because they reproduce many traditional institution features, but by putting to work distributed ledger technology. Intrinsically, these projects symbolize noncompliance with the networks of power, and advocate for self-administration.

As I noted before, a layer code draws an invisible link between Fluxus and Dada, with conceptual artists and their set of instructions. All of those works are based on the execution of rules.[75] The same impetus is replicated in an NFT. The avant-garde practices focused investigations on the medium, whether it was through materials like television, or the lack thereof, such as in a Happening. However, artists working with blockchains emphasize experimentation with distribution networks. The capacity to execute rules is engrained on a code level through smart contracts, and tokenization facilitates new structures of belonging, which I will explain in chapter 3.

As a result, artists working with blockchains concentrate on how their artworks can provide new forms of interaction and connection between different nodes, agents, and access points, and how they can steer their behavior and expectations toward the future. It could be by creating a DAO like the venture capital–backed Friends with Benefits, which the *New York Times* described as "a kind of digital co-op that uses cryptocurrency tokens to coordinate access, make payments and vote on group decisions."[76] Or it could be something like the Bread Cooperative, which is a community of decentralized, cooperatives projects building development tools that help forge solidarity between individuals and collectives.[77] The technology is used to sustain a kin infrastructure among the participants, meaning that experimentation concentrates on how the community is built, stewarded, *distributed*. These types of projects thus maintain the same spirit: the desire for rupture and the craving for a different social imaginary, one where personal monetary profit is not the basis of exchange: it is social surplus. Yet, the tactics deployed by the traditional avant-garde differ, as blockchain artists emphasize experimentation with chains of distribution as part of the artistic medium.

Take the DAO *Holly+*, a project led by composer Holly Herndon in collaboration with Never Before Heard Sounds. They created a voice model, which is a deep neural network (an AI) that can generate an audio based on an individual voice, in this case Herndon's natural voice. Anyone can upload an audio of music to their website and receive a download of that music sung back with her voice. It functions like a deepfake, but here, instead of instead of infringing copyright laws, the artist is giving it away for free, as a commons, to continue expanding experimentation. Like the earlier avant-garde movement, *Holly+* challenges and ruptures with the past, represented here in the traditional notion of digital identity associated with one person, who could potentially monetize their own data. *Holly+* offers a new form of stewardship for the voice model, which deploys a DAO, meaning that the ownership is decentralized. That is to say, it experiments with distribution, which makes free the ultimately always human voice into a disembodied nonhuman asset that can be used to continue inquiring about possible uses of AI in music creation. The DAO can vote for, approve, and certify new works employing the voice model. It also manages the funds stemming from usage, and with those funds it supports the development of new tools. The token holders of the DAO *Holly+* help with the quality control, as they vote on works using the voice model. This mechanism helps improve the value of the project as a whole and also imposes certain quality standards on its descendants. It also provokes is a more-than-human-kin relation between the members of the DAO as they are united to collectively safeguard the best possible outcome for the nonhuman voice model. Value here is not related to any monetary transaction. The cycle of worth dissemination is relational to the community that decides on it through the DAO. As a result, the project provides a new way to distribute an artistic feature (the voice in this case) and to facilitate the development of new AI tools for composition along with fostering creativity, unconstrained by traditional copyright laws that are not adapted to the radically different texture created by the spawn of AI.

The notion of collectivity was always present in avant-garde practice. Yet, as curator Gavin Grindon explains, it had entirely unique outputs.[78] While the Russian Constructivists became official engineers of the Soviet Union,[79] the Dadaists and Surrealists strove to renew art outside the boundaries of the institution, abandoning waged labor to encourage new forms of collective existence.[80] The intention was nonetheless the same for both: to merge the realms of art and life into one that would make the bourgeois institution of art, considered the paradigm of autonomy, disappear. One can observe that trend in the plethora of platforms providing blockchains specifically for creatives. Zora,[81] Metalabel,[82] or Outland[83] present themselves as a way to democratize access, providing an alternative to traditional players in the art world. They propose an alternative to the neoliberal order (here embodied in the art world), which empowers the creators of the artwork to revert extraction that often occurs in the moment of selling and/or distribution by generating a community-based organization.

These ventures are gestures that grapple with the machinery of the capitalist market, and also provide glimpses of the world-building potential of blockchain.

Barbara Cueto: You have worked with different artists and curators, so I would like to ask you what do these artistic practices bring to diverse economic systems?

Katherine Gibson: The artists that we've been involved [with] are doing incredible experimentation in a kind of an economic way. Really, they're trying to get people together to think, work, and produce differently. So that kind of creativity around economic experimentation is something that I think artists are bringing to the project of building community economies. Certainly not just about the representations that they produce, that are nice and pretty, and they are very important in terms of communication too. But I think about it as a form of freedom. I mean, it's . . . an impoverished freedom. I know all the artists are living off hardly anything.

In a way, artists have already decided "I'm going to do this because I'm interested in it even if it doesn't make me a living at that." I think that gives them the freedom to experiment in sorts of very unexpected ways, which I think is really helpful for social scientists and others, who are sort of more stuck in traditional research. It's a different way of

> learning that is very important for unleashing creativity, and unleashing trust amongst people, which is very important for any building of new economies. So I think . . . it's crucial. I'd like to see all research grants have a role for an artist built into them. Because it does expand your thinking, you know? It's been interesting how many artists are attracted to our work. And it's been very gratifying. We've learned a lot from it, too.

The avant-garde stressed the relation between collectivity with struggle, opposing the individualized realm of aesthetic appreciation represented by art institutions.[84] They managed, as Massimiliano Mollona suggests, to "at least suspend the logic of capitalism" and inhabit a grey zone that "valorised instead the speculative, conceptual and immaterial labour."[85] This value emerged performatively, relying on contact between the artwork and the public.[86] This performative notion of value is also present in many blockchain art projects, since a token, as a proxy for value, is of worth only to the holder and its community that proportionally allocates members' resources to maintain it. Let's consider Channel, which is a decentralized media organization composed of Interdependence (Mat Dryhurst and Holly Herndon), New Models (Caroline Busta and Lil Internet), and Joshua Citarella. Channel is also a platform that "allows creators to use Web3 tools to work collectively, bundling content while maintaining distinct communities."[87] Channel, as a DAO, created 666 NFTs, which cost 880 USD each. Holding a token means to participate in the project's early development along with getting access to its podcast feed. The NFTs were all sold within a couple of days. Severin Matusek, who is a holder of one of these NFTs, explains quite clearly why having one is meaningful: it gives you access, entails participation, creates belonging, becomes a form of status, and acts as a speculative asset.[88] The community, therefore, becomes the asset.[89]

+Life is a dApp created by Voiz DAO (now Kith Climate), which is a climate justice organization that trains Gen Z students to become sustainability analysts through exercises in writing sustainability-focused reviews of companies and products.[90] Tailored to their community, the design studio Neo-Metabolism developed a concept and demo for a digital product. +Life is intended to guide sustainable investments for the Voiz community by aggregating sustainability assessments created by its own members. Carsten Goertz, a member of Neo-Metabolism,[91] explained that "it aims to demonstrate how our ideas about kinship technology can bring utopian communities into effect towards real-world change, while interfacing with the financial system."[92] The technology becomes the social glue uniting users in an alternative collective value system, namely their desire to build a sustainable future that materializes in a responsible portfolio. The community is the project's main asset, and the provider of shared knowledge from which each individual benefits.

Barbara Cueto: Could the art world be the right place to start a movement of movements?

Geert Lovink: Artworks are very important when it comes to experimentation. Arts and culture have the freedom to think about solutions, alternatives, visions, and pleasures. The role of visual, auditive, or performative ways [of art is] to express why we're doing all this in the first place, right? There's a utopian element in it because there is still always about some kind of other world being possible, and also it can be celebrated here on the spot, together. That is what gives the artists a lot of energy, and, eventually, also many more people that participate in it.

In the case of Critical Blockchain Art, the artists, who tend to work in collectives due to the projects' complexity, strive to foster the being-with of Nancy.[93] Their works execute a type of world-building organized through social surplus, moving flawlessly between realms, producing hand-on games, workshops, or live-action role-playing (LARP) that come to enact their digital counterpart (to be explained further). They blur the distinction between life and art to propose alternative social arrangements that question the logic of surplus capitalism, *Liquid Dependencies*, the Sphere, Channel, or Dayra. In this way, the participants can experience the capacity of blockchain to implicitly readdress power relations.[94] Critical Blockchain Art holds the same impulse that joins art and life, following the lineage from the modernist avant-garde to Fluxus, on through AIDS Coalition to Unleash Power (ACT UP) and Occupy Wall Street.[95] Concretely, the Occupy movement emphasized embodied experiences of sight, sound, and touch to present political claims against the status quo. The artistic practices that happened around the movement helped construct a collective imaginary that exceeds the museological enclosure, where art was understood as political force.[96]

Artists experimenting with blockchains express the same motivations and their works dissolve the boundaries between life and art to explore new forms of living and being in the world. Long before them, Fluxus famously led a series of interdisciplinary projects with different U.S. scientific, technological, and industrial innovation companies and universities. The investigations led to the dissolution of the author and the rise of the spectator. Collaterally, these experiences attempted to "initiate new modes of inquiry unfettered by conventional distinctions based on professional loyalties, prejudices, or habits of mind."[97]

These experiments dim the borders between art and life to unleash creativity from artists and scientists. In the case of Critical Blockchain Art, by proposing alternative social imaginaries with new forms of governance, these projects present a different way of living that is a reaction to the individualizing forces of neoliberalism. Technologists, developers, and artists work together and pool resources to generate a new social infrastructure to support their own version of emancipation. The utopian challenge to the existing state of affairs re-emerges in consecutive timeframes, experimenting with formats and mediums and, now, with distribution channels. Critical Blockchain Art is, I argue, the newest embodiment of the longing for subversion of the avant-garde transforming the notion of value. Using postcapitalist vocabularies, these collectivizing, praxis-oriented artworks convey radical sociopolitical imaginaries grounded on non-capitalocentric lexicons that gesture toward new possibilities and the urgent desire for transformation. Of course, they remain entangled in the structures they seek to challenge, as the technology itself is embedded in the logic of capital. But it is precisely in this tension that their force lies. They do not claim to fully escape, but to question, reimagine, and redirect. They work within the contradictions, shaping tools to rethink what is possible. And it is in this careful, persistent reworking of the conditions we inherit that I find hope.

The Influence of Beuys's Social Sculpture

Following in the steps of the avant-garde and Fluxus, Joseph Beuys developed the notion of social sculpture ("Soziale Plastik"), understood as the dynamics of universal connectivity between natural materials, artifacts, humans, and even animals and plants.[98] Art and life are in a continuum, again, as they were for the artists of the avant-garde. As Joseph Beuys famously said, everyone is an artist, meaning that life and art are not separate but inextricably linked. Again, then, collectivity and hope, features of the avant-garde, resurface in Beuys and are also present in Critical Blockchain Art. The productive fluidity of Beuys's concept of social sculpture provides a valuable access point to approach the nature of these distributed ledger technology practices. Critical Blockchain Art extends some of these principles, entangling technology and users, giving agency to humans and nonhumans and creating structures of belonging. These structures create kinship relationships between participants through a collective process of knowledge production and dissemination.

As curator and long-term collaborator Caroline Tisdall explains, for Beuys, art included the entire process of living, including thoughts, actions, and dialogue as well as objects, and, therefore, it could be enacted by all people.[99] Beuys was influenced by Fluxus and the avant-garde: on the one hand, Fluxus bypassed the art institution with event-based practices that activated viewers; on the other, the avant-garde succeeded in overcoming the regulation of bourgeois state institutions and in lifting limitations on their creativity, opening up to all images and forms.[100] As a result, Beuys theorized sculpture as a changing principle, or a thrust of energy that could reshape society.[101]

The first manifestation of Beuys's concept of social sculpture took place during Documenta in 1972, where he showed *Office for Direct Democracy*. This work was set up as an office where Beuys and two assistants discussed, with whomever would come, the possibility of average people initiating public policy. Beuys believed that social sculpture could "mould and shape the world in which we live" and, hence, affect social change.[102] In his lecture *The Society as Artwork*,[103] Beuys suggested replacing modern society with "a pure form of a self-organised social organism, as it will come to life in the future."[104] This prefigurative inspiration comes from a firm belief in self-determination, which translated into a commitment with direct democracy.[105] Social sculpture has, therefore, an active nature. It functions as an active space, "as a social centre, as a laboratory of the communal and a site for aesthetic experiments."[106] In it, actions and demonstrations could be adapted and changed.[107] The audience members, likewise, become active subjects, not in the sense of interactive art but as collaborators in the process of meaning-making through collective responsibility.[108] Traditional notions of authorship and spectatorship are, consequently, challenged.

Intrinsically, these projects not only represent noncompliance with the networks of power, they also advocate for self-administration. They introduce an antagonistic discourse, which, consequently, positions them even further from relational aesthetics, as Bishop's earlier comment indicates.[109] As with Beuys's oeuvre, the "creative imperative addressed the possibility of humans shaping the living environment—in terms of freedom, self-determination and a kind of postmaterialistic economy."[110] Critical Blockchain Art uses creativity and imagination, blending art and life to propose an alternative way of living, supported by cooperating agents in a nonhierarchical manner.

Autonomous Forest as a Social Sculpture

Ownership of forest land in Germany is unevenly distributed: 48 percent is privately owned, 29 percent is owned by the federal states, 19 percent by companies, and 4 percent by the federal government. In a country of 349,223 square kilometers, there are almost no *public* or communal forests. Moreover, years of exploitation as timber production has made most of the forests a monoculture, making them less resilient to pests and with lower indicators of biodiversity. In response to this, in 2016 Paul Kolling and Paul Seidler's artists collective terra0 proposed a self-owned forest. This speculative forest would be able to sell licenses to cut trees through automated processes and blockchain technology. As a result, the forest would accumulate capital, enabling it to eventually own itself. After a long prototyping phase, I curated *Autonomous Forest* as an R&D project for LAS Art Foundation in Berlin. It launched in

November 2025 as a regeneration project, becoming the first forest in Germany managed under a DAO structure and holding legal standing under German law. The mission remained the same: to remove ecosystems from the economic sphere and allow them to regenerate autonomously.

Autonomous Forest takes forest land out of circulation to both prevent any commercial use and allow it to regenerate. The forest's legal framework is a *verein,* the German word for an association of people united by a common interest or goal. *Vereine* (plural) in Germany abound: they could be soccer clubs, nonprofits, or NGOs. The verein gives the DAO legal capacity under German civil law; and the blockchain infrastructure underpins the system with transparency, irreversibility, and inclusive decision-making. The sale of NFTs provides funds to the verein to acquire more forest land, and gives the members of the DAO/verein decision-making power on possible administrative tasks. As a result, *Autonomous Forest* produces a techno-ecological assemblage that endows autonomy to the living forest, continuing Beuys's desire for self-determination, which permeated his social sculpture project.

Autonomous Forest's tokens have a double function: as an NFT, it holds digital artworks describing the topology of the forest; as a membership token, it endows the token holder with voting power. The project functions as a living land art project that harnesses Web3 to foster new forms of engagement of a translocal community stewarding a nonhuman asset. The token holders collectively own the forest and oversee its organization using a blockchain as a governance mechanism. This socio-technical assemblage redefines ownership itself, shifting from financial extraction to a nonprofit, regenerative model of forest management. This shift in perspective establishes a more-than-human community in a project of regenerative commons: it is an experiment in shared responsibility. Here, blockchain is not a speculative tool but a connective infrastructure. It binds participants in a shared experiment in postcapitalist governance, care, and critique, while openly challenging the logic of capitalist forest exploitation in Germany.

The smart contract carries a double function. Unstaked, the NFTs map specific parcels of forest and generate an artwork that responds to the plot's topology. Staked, these NFTs become membership tokens that unlock voting rights. The number of governance tokens an NFT yields depends on its age in years plus the chosen staking period (governance tokens = NFT age + staking period). For instance, staking a newly minted NFT for five years generates five governance tokens, while staking one created four years ago for the same period generates twenty. This simple formula rewards long-term commitment and care, aligning economic interests with ecological preservation. Acting as kin tokens, the smart contract forms a connective tissue with the community, whose members pursue a collective goal of ecological regeneration. In this way, *Autonomous Forest* shifts value from speculation to participation, transforming stewardship itself into a form of collective wealth.

Through this polymorphic aesthetic experiment, the *Autonomous Forest* audience members became active participants. The same active principle can be found in social sculptures. This medium makes the audience part of the underlying process of knowledge production encompassed in their own conceptual development. This means that there is also a flexibility, as social sculptures change according to the audience's influence.[111] The DAO/verein is also flexible, enabling response to potential changes at an infrastructure level, such as new members or ecological factors, such as wildfires or droughts, which would require it to act differently in their theory of regeneration. In this way, *Autonomous Forest* condenses Beuys's notion of the active space. The artwork's adaptive capacity is guaranteed by the governance structure afforded by the technology.

Beuys's social sculpture avowed that anyone who would like to change society for the better could do so by exercising creativity, with or without being an artist. For him, art becomes the creative means to construct conversations, generate collective practices, and support new forms of organization.[112] terra0 extends these ideas and broadens the role of Beuys's "universal connectivity"[113] to include nonhumans in their proposal, taking this position to enact change through art. In doing so, *Autonomous Forest* becomes a tool for activism that advocates regeneration against the exploitation of ecological resources. The DAO/verein hopes to set both ethical and legal precedents in Germany. First, to encourage a conversation about natural personhood and collective stewardship that could help inform debates about the ethics of forest management, conservation, land ownership, and rights of nature. And second, to create a legal basis to weave the German verein legal entity into the Web3 DAO. With this double gesture, *Autonomous Forest* encapsulates Beuys's support for direct democracy and his commitment to self-determination.[114] As Erika Biddle puts it, for Beuys, "Art becomes techne for realising democracy."[115] And, in the same way, terra0 continues his legacy including the technology-driven proposal that updates the contemporary debates about the role of art in society.

CONCLUSION

It is hard to explain (and even harder to root in a discourse) a new art form that is still growing and developing. Not only is the technology being perfected, but also practitioners are only now starting to properly practice, becoming fluent in this language of subversion. We are somewhere after the frenzied postfinancial bubble, and hopefully heading toward a golden age. Examples are still few, but they all point to a radically new way of understanding. Critical Blockchain Art's tentacles spread between disciplines and methodologies, because a community (radically) imagines their social existence based on a complete transformation and, collaterally, debates the legitimacy of the previous imaginary by challenging it with community members' own.

Critical Blockchain Art challenges, like digital art before it, classic models of display, mediation, and reproduction of traditional art. In conjunction, it encourages expanded versions of spectatorship, production, and collaboration, as did socially engaged art. The critique is strengthened because it can circumvent the art process of valorization and commodification, since these projects are more independent of the existing networks.[116] Furthermore, like the critical digital artworks, Critical Blockchain Art is grounded on long investigations that inquire into the repercussions of neoliberalism in the postdigital realm, and respond with new forms of engagement that overcome the physical/virtual dichotomy. As a result, they enhance the project of institutional critique and provide a new medium for social practice.

Chapter 2 analyzed the critical potential of digital art from the perspectives of institutional critique and socially engaged art, leaving aside the more traditional investigations related to the aesthetics of new media. Both frameworks coincide in the enhanced criticality endowed to digital art thanks to their independence from the art systems of valorization and their success overcoming its commodification. Moreover, because of their techno-cultural complex awareness, they can reach beyond the museum and problematize the power structures and oppression of postdigital societies at large. Consequently, digital art exercises a richer form of institutional critique and provides a new medium for social practices that fosters a wider sense of postdigital community. The critical potential of digital practices resides in their new ways of engaging with our contemporary algorithmic reality, making socially engaged art more aware and attuned to the effects and desires of a post-digital society.

Digital art at large is nested in different constellations of agents and powers, avoiding the misuses of socially engaged art at museums, and the over-institutionalization of critique. Its nature questions the traditional structures of the art system, as it calls into question conventional methods of ownership, interaction, distribution, and participation. By minimizing its dependence, it also holds a new sense of agency and fosters new manners of engagement. It expands the notion of spectatorship and dismantles authorship as a mere process.[117] Transformation is a dual process that involves the agents cooperating in the development and the participating audience because of their political engagement.[118] These conditions stimulate new forms of interaction both inside the making of art and with the art system that, consequently, exceed museological rationale. Digital art thereby confronts the very nature of these institutions at large, raising questions regarding their function in terms of display, mediation, and reproduction.

In particular, socially engaged digital practices share their immateriality, adaptability of physical compositions, and wide online reach, making them more independent from the constraints of art institutions. They are also concerned with fostering social change and offer alternatives to the systems of algorithmic oppression.[119] Socially engaged digital artworks emphasize a communal experience that transforms the participants into coauthors in a process of transversal and transnational, online and offline collaboration. They embody the same systemic form of critique, often involving the politics of digital commons. In contrast to institutional critique, they share the same focus as social practices: the creation of a community as a response to neoliberal policies.[120] The online and offline cooperation of these participatory digital artworks is, therefore, a political gesture, which sets them apart from relational aesthetics.

These artistic practices provide moments of world-building that enact the same utopian longing, desire for rupture, and craving for a new society of the avant-garde. Yet, here, they emerge by means of experimentation with distribution channels. In Beuys's terminology, they convey an expanded notion of art, dissolving the spheres of art and other human activities. They enact, through direct action, the power of creativity to shape new living environments that give rise to today's utopias. Critical Blockchain Art embodies the same characteristics but expands the forms of collaboration and offers an experimental take on the technology. These practices make possible a type of commons-oriented social coordination that allocates worth to social surplus instead of accumulation of capital. The creativity to adapt its affordances allows practitioners of Critical Blockchain Art to convey their own version of utopia.

3 CRITICAL BLOCKCHAIN ART

Barbara Cueto: In 2004 you asked in a text about interventionist art: "Can you have a revolutionary art without a revolution?" Twenty years after this, is this question still relevant?

Gregory Sholette: I guess there's two questions: what is revolutionary? And then the second is, what does art have to do with revolution? When I wrote that, I had the second question in mind. It was a moment when a lot of artists were suddenly becoming very interested in making work that was fairly political, certainly social in its nature and public, moving out of the gallery, and doing work that was often not so much [an] expression of a specific politics, but trying to interrupt everyday life in a way that actually made people hopefully think about how life might be improved, or how it might change or how it might need to change. It was not like Surrealism, where you would just interrupt the reality with something extraordinary or profane, or unexpected. For a long time, artists had not been deeply political, I'm talking about [the] late 1980s and 1990s. At that time, there was an interest in representation. And this would be considered somehow political. Whereas this work that was emerging in the late 1990s and early 2000s, which we call Interventionism, was related to Tactical Media, and was trying to go into the streets and make something happen. That

> raised the question for me: can you have all these interesting interventions add up to something that might be considered real social change? And this comes back to the first question, what is revolution? I then intended it to mean a really fundamental social change, social, political, and economic change at a fundamental level. A thumbnail sketch of what revolution is would be rupture and change that moves towards [a] new direction. And hopefully, in a better direction, where there's more equality, less oppression, more resources. It's a very old-fashioned idea, it is really a nineteenth century, or even eighteenth century idea of revolution. But what [does] revolution mean today? We have a particular narrative, and it's very linear about what changes.
>
> In a way, I was not completely buying the Interventionist idea, but I thought it was exciting. When I asked people what is the ultimate, social objective, there was never really an answer. Where does that take us politically? How is this different than operating as an NGO? You never really changed the system, you just throw more band-aids on the system. You alleviate suffering to some degree, but you never actually get to the underlying circumstances. And that was the question I was asking. . . . How can you have a revolutionary art without a revolution?

In recent years, art has gained prominence in movements like Occupy, as embodied practices have become ever more important in promoting engagement.[1] Artistic practices have presented political claims against the status quo that help build up the collective imaginary of the social movement.[2] As a result, art reinvents its function beyond museological enclosure; it becomes a new kind of political force. It is radical imagination that makes us question how we live, as Yates McKee posits.[3]

Chapters 1 and 2 established blockchain as a site for place-based politics, a terrain where the very notion of value can be reimagined. I also traced the genealogy of Critical Blockchain Art within art history. Chapter 3 turns to Critical Blockchain Art's political agency. Here, artistic practices of dissent emerge as speculative performances in which artists and allied communities anticipate the contours of a society yet to come, since they can engender a new, digital, and decentralized site for place-based politics. And that is precisely their counterpower: the capacity to pre-enact in the present, the future that they long for.

But I need to start by disentangling three convoluted concepts: radical imagination, utopia, and prefiguration. Together, they form the conceptual weave that situates blockchain within emancipatory politics and aligns it with the legacy of new social movements. From this ground, I develop a language of autonomy, emancipation, and political agency that privileges embodied experience over abstract theory. Here I explain three notions that describe what blockchain-mediated communities experience, which are the key to Critical Blockchain Art: dislocated time, structures of belonging, and infrastructures of critique. It is here that art's political agency unfolds: in the weaving of counter-hegemonic projects that do not propose a single horizon, but rather open onto a constellation of possible worlds, a multiverse of agonistic futures.

THE RADICAL IMAGINATION TO CREATE BLOCKCHAIN

Radical imagination is about thinking the world differently. Yet it is more than that, as it is also about "bringing those possible futures back to work on the present, to inspire action and new forms of solidarity today," as pointed out by social justice scholars Max Haiven and Alex Khasnabish.[4] Radical imagination is an active process involving both present and future, emphasizing collectivity in a translocal manner. It "undergirds our capacity to build solidarity across boundaries and borders, real or imagined."[5] This practice of imagination is deemed radical because it is a reaction to "deeply rooted tensions, contradictions, power imbalances, and forms of oppression and exploitation" as Haiven and Khasnabish point out. But, most importantly, it intends to trigger a profound transformation in the beliefs that ground the system itself. Without radical imagination, I believe, the type of blockchain infrastructures I talked about wouldn't exist.

According to philosopher Cornelius Castoriadis, although social forms appear to be permanent, they are only a temporary solidification of a shared radical imagination. He calls it "Magma" to represent the ever-changing nature of an imaginary. An imaginary is collectively conceived and organizes the imagination and the symbolism of the political.[6] For Castoriadis, instead of a value judgment, radical imagination is an analytical category or a sociological process. In his view, it is related to the production of images that precede any thought and is related to two German concepts: *Einbildung*, as in fantasy or imagination, and *Bilder*, which means images. However, radical imagination does not create images in a visual sense so much as a general one, which linguists would refer to as an acoustic image of a word.[7] This implies a link between pictures and images to political imaginaries, since they are connected to types of imagination. "They are manifestations of the imaginary while they motivate modes of perception and types of imagination," assert Craig Browne and Paula Diehl.[8]

Barbara Cueto: If blockchain becomes the infrastructure holding autonomous organizations, what are the things that blockchain could potentially be better suited for doing?

Geert Lovink: Blockchain facilitates the redistribution of wealth. It is an administrative ledger, yes. But you can do so many more things with it, and that's just why so many people entered this realm. Not because we all aspire to be financial

> administrators but because it is the possibility to blow up that old idea of accounting. Let's talk about what would be a fair twenty-first-century version of accounting. Because it's so vital. That's the original motivation. And, unfortunately, the story has now developed and some newcomers might have another idea about it. But then it's up to us to tell and retell that story, the origin, the myth in the most positive sense.

Composing a new social imaginary is a political task with symbolic power, and it is formulated through acoustic images of a future world created with a shared radical imagination. Either fostering knowledge-commons production or creating a care network, blockchain is an adaptable tool that radical imagination can put to work to generate alternative social imaginaries articulated through technological means. If we go back to the Yin Aiwen's game, *Liquid Dependencies*, it enacted a non-capitalocentric social imaginary, where the participants collectively performed their life *as if* they live in that utopia that used blockchain as their social infrastructure. Although the game would not make sense without the technology's capacity for queering value, the game functions independently, the project of the creation of a new lexicon of economic existence that rests in the background, as a collective imaginary is slowly constructed through the different LARP exercises. The technology is only a tool that activates the radical imagination of the participants. The gameplay allows us to consider our own existence and choices, as one imagines living another social imaginary. This is not an isolated case; the previously mentioned conference "Beyond Cultures of Ownership: Emerging Strategies for Interdependence" represents a new interest in art beyond its aesthetic form, art as a productive field of research that could overcome the limits of traditional science. The conference reflected on the art world's ability to envision alternative forms of property and imagine the ripple effects on licensing, governance, commons management, or sustainability.[9] Programs like this reinforce the newly acquired value of the art world as prototyping realm for forward-thinking imaginaries that now find themselves on the borderline between artistic practice and start-up community.

"Social imaginary" is a broad term that encompasses the ways in which people imagine their social existence. It is a "common understanding that makes possible common practices and a widely shared sense of legitimacy."[10] The political potential of blockchain relies on its capacity to shape and envision a social imaginary. Imagination becomes, in turn, constitutional and constituent. It "is a practice that is not only potentially practical in its effects, but also purposeful in its intentions: polemical and problem-solving at the same time."[11] This means that this type of imagination can affect the social imaginary of popular sovereignty, along with helping to generate a sense of anticipation at a moment of struggle. As a result, an imaginary also stands as a form to consider the world into being, opening a new space where imagination "can be understood as a temporary site of resistance and alterity."[12]

Blockchain social imaginaries are evocative and transformative because they create different images of worlds with alternative social production according to specific collective desires. They join, in this way, critical and resolute features, as they implicitly challenge the legitimacy of the existing imaginary by challenging it with their own version of utopia.

UTOPIAN FUTURES ON BLOCKCHAIN

I cannot start without stating the obvious: this all has an aftertaste of utopia. Instead of simply continuing blockchain's potential for financialization to expand into new, previously non-financialized spheres, I believe that Web3 can also offer an alternative social structure that does not prioritize the market. These techno-social compositions are organized around the fostering of the community, the being-with recalled by Nancy. And, in this way, the compositions give rise to counter-hegemonic orders.

Although utopia doesn't convey exactly either the sentiment or the emancipatory potential hosted with the synthetic infrastructure of blockchain, it is important to remember the impulse behind utopia. The three great utopian thinkers—Henri de Saint-Simon, Joseph Fourier, and Robert Owen—located the outset of utopia in the absolute break with the established order. They tried to enfranchise humans by presenting them with utopian images of a new world with radically different social relations that open a new path away from capitalism. Blockchain imaginaries act similarly, presenting themselves as a rupture with the previous order that triggered the global financial crisis of 2008 known as the Great Recession, offering an acoustic image of a world post-crisis, and formulating paths toward emancipation.

Barbara Cueto: We were very optimistic and probably very naive at the beginning of the internet; and we are at a similar moment again, both with AI and blockchain. At the same time, we are experiencing a collateral wave of misinformation and censorship that comes from Web 2.0.

Gregory Sholette: That's a really interesting point you make about waves of optimism, followed by realism, followed by skepticism and cynicism, followed by optimism. Maybe that is something to think about in terms of technology, or maybe even just in modern life. Obviously, revolutionary enthusiasm turns very dark. We see what happened with [the] Enlightenment or the Soviet Union. Maybe these waves are what we mean when we talk about revolution.

> Instead of revolution in the sense of a break, we think of revolution as what it actually literally means, which is to spin around. And this comes back to the question of progress. Because there's no point in having a revolution unless there's a moment of progress over what occurred before. Why are we going to get rid of the old if it's not going to be improved? Maybe the concept of progress is part of the problem here because we assumed there has to be this narrative called progress. And then when it fails us, progress becomes incredibly cynical and dark. And that's the moment we're in right now for sure.

According to Uri Gordon, generations ago, the future was an affective space traditionally composed of expectant optimism; however, nowadays, we all feel it differently. The future we see is filled with anxiety, bitterness, and culpability.[13] This texture of feeling also affects the structure of utopia. One cannot feel but disenchanted when we look at our politicians today, or disempowered when we see election results across the world. Utopia is always linked to a desire for change and has an ethical approach.[14] This means that descriptions of social arrangements are not what stimulates a revision of a hegemonic order; rather, it is the exploration of values that is undertaken.[15] Ernst Bloch relates the notion of hope to the impulse for social action, considering that concrete imaginings are able "to extend, in an anticipating way, existing material into the future possibilities of being different and better."[16] Hence, the future is the beholder of that hope; but what can its role be in this anxiety-filled future?

Bloch's principle of hope, which comes from the affective and powerful idea of the "not-yet," requires a reformulation. Heidegger noted that anxiety holds the potential for enlightenment, since it is the first experience of freedom, a manifestation that conceives and reconceives the world in many ways.[17] Recognizing the present anxiety as the first symptom of emancipation reshapes the feeling into a tool that triggers a search to think and construct an alternative future. Similar notions can be found elsewhere; for example, in the research on sustainability activists in Turkey. Anthropologist Bürge Abiral points out that "instead of being an opposite of hope, anxiety is a companion to it. . . . The anxiety that they feel about the future accompanies their hopeful condition and all the more pushes them to act in the present."[18] And that is why I believe that many of the projects using blockchains are born out of that anxious hope that started in a sudden distrust of fiat money during the Great Recession in 2008. Distributed ledger technology brought hope to the community that sees in the technology a way to escape that hegemonic order and, most importantly, it provides an alternative that can be practiced today. This anchoring in the present makes it a form of concrete utopianism, far from an abstract one, which Ruth Levitas describes as hieratic social blueprints or personal daydreams.[19] If we understand Web3 in these terms, blockchain is able to update Bloch's principle of hope but with a Heideggerian anxiety.

People understand utopia in different ways. I like to think of it as a simulacrum, influenced by the writing of philosopher Miguel Abensour who states that utopia holds "an effect of resemblance by different means than the model: it is built upon a disparity and this enables it to liberate difference from all subordination to the similar and the identical."[20] Web3 is driven by the same utopian desire for a break with the established order and a desire to trigger action. The technology provides a space of alterity using lex cryptographica, the private regulatory frameworks that operate on each blockchain, which can create any type of regulation that will be implemented on the governance infrastructure of a blockchain organization. Lex cryptographica operates on an ex-ante temporal matrix, which entails predesigning the future. Since the norms are implemented and enforced beforehand, the future is already defined in the present through the set of rules that will be applied. Lex cryptographica creates a de facto simulacrum. It imitates the feeling of prefiguration, the timeless time described by Castells. This simulacrum is never singular because technology can be endlessly reconfigured to support any potential configuration of utopia. For Abensour, utopia is a form of "seduction, a stimulus to present action"[21] that acts in the realm of affectivity. Analogously, distributed ledger technology not only proposes an alternative social imaginary, but also helps bring it about. Without imagination, we cannot envision where to move forward. Simulacrum acts as a crack that opens outward toward new futures. "The simulacrum is a rupture with the world of essences, forms, or norms: it opens a new career to becoming and makes possible the invention of the new."[22] This recursive movement creates an imaginary of *elsewheres* and *otherwises* that draw into the affective nature of the desire for change.

How can a synthetic digital apparatus be so human as an affective essence of the feeling of autonomy? I think blockchain achieves this because it updates Bloch's principle of hope with Heideggerian anxiety. New non-capitalocentric blockchain structures are responses toward anxious hope, which reciprocally bestows its community with hope. It can constitute a space for alterity and, as was argued in chapter 1, becomes the locus for a place-based politics. But we need to reappropriate, reconstruct, and reinvent blockchain, as Harcourt proposes.[23] If we leave it to the perils of the market, blockchain technology will inevitably be co-opted to do what blockchain is best at: creating new surfaces of extraction. That is to say, the technology functions as a seduction of a future social order by proposing a social imaginary implemented on its lex cryptographica. These new social imaginaries are harnessed to the immutability, rigidity, and permanence of the legal-institutional framework anchored on blockchains. It is a rupture and a path. And it is also a call for action. Blockchain makes possible new utopias that work as a simulacrum, producing as many *elsewheres* as disaffections today.

Barbara Cueto: In an interview, you said "My brain may be a pessimist but my heart remains an optimist." How do you feel now (2024) about blockchain? Can we still look at this technology in a positive light?

Geert Lovink: I am positive because distributed digital ledgers will fit into the larger picture. If we are going to see [blockchain] only as something in itself, then forget about it. If we see it as a vital tool for the redistribution of value it will be a key part of working toward a fairer world or society. If you're a materialist, like me, you know the importance of economics and monetary systems and the devastating impact they can have on the lives of ordinary people. If you don't, there is a straight-out risk of nationalism, racism, and fascism.

DECRYPTING CRITICAL BLOCKCHAIN ART

The idea of a social imaginary might be slightly elusive to some. The same goes for prefiguration and perhaps even utopia. How can these apply to this new practice of Critical Blockchain Art? What would this look like? I have located its roots in the spirit of rupture and craving for a new society of the avant-garde; in the comprehensive and nuanced analysis related to institutional critique; in the commitment to support a translocal community arising from socially engaged practices; and in the workings of a peer-to-peer support network of digital activism. However, positioned at the intersection of art and technological experimentation, Critical Blockchain Art is, indeed, a slippery term. This type of project is much more than just a continuation of socially engaged projects or institutional critique. It is also different from but profoundly influenced by the workings of digital activism. Heterogenous in form, topics, and reach, these artistic projects coincide in that they radically imagine an alternative to the existing conditions. Be it a tool for sustainable investing in the shape of a dApp like +Life, a DAO that rethinks creativity and copyright like *Holly+*, or an NFT marketplace to support live art developed by the Sphere, this new art form helps think and consider how blockchain could become an agent of change. It offers the experience of the otherwise world, of the as-if politics, of a future that might never become real. That is why these practices are relevant today, especially in these bleak times, because Critical Blockchain Art embodies a new architecture of aesthetic resistance. How does this movement do this? Through three interlocking processes, which I have pointed out throughout this book: Critical Blockchain Art dislocates time; it generates a structure of belonging for communities; and this structure of belonging bestows on communities an infrastructure of critique.

Dislocated Time

Dislocated time refers to the weird temporal matrix discussed earlier with regard to prefiguration, timeless time, and simulacrum. It is a productive asset in the language of imagination because it replaces the temporal separation between today's struggle and future goals. The gesture of thinking of the world *as-if*, or of LARPing a world where we would like to live through a technological apparatus, is the cornerstone of the functioning of Critical Blockchain Art. In it, lex cryptographica hard-codes the temporality in which we can design the future in the present. In becoming rehearsals of the *not-yet*, the act of dislocating time can improve and avoid the many pitfalls, to create better technologies that could enable better societies. This temporal hiccup grants political agency, prototyping futures through the practice of today. It becomes what Noël Sturgeon calls "direct theory," as it theorizes through action.[24] As a result, the affordances of the technology make possible a type of social experimentation that would be otherwise impossible, as Critical Blockchain Art uses the technical possibilities to generate new social structures based on communal actions that foster social surplus.

Prefiguration emphasizes direct implementation, thereby replacing the temporal separation between the struggle of today and goals in the future. In turn, renewed consideration of utopia often revolves around imagining/creating autonomous spaces with different social relationships, providing a texture of feeling that moves beyond the despair of capitalism to become the productive notion of anxious hope. Prefiguration is a bit different, because it is an interplay between theory and practice that creates alternatives in the here and now. As political theorist Ruth Kinna argues, the two notions are not opposed, as the dreams and visions of utopia are still embedded in the different strands of prefigurative actions.[25] Rather, their entwinement can be observed in the various definitions of prefiguration. For example, Steve Buechler explains that the "pursuit of utopian goals is recursively built into the movement's daily operation and organizational style,"[26] and John Carter and Dave Morland refer to prefiguration as "a strategy that is an embryonic representation of an anarchist social future."[27] Prefiguration shares foundational aspects with utopia and anarchism, although it has a practice-oriented nature. Blockchain uses the ex-ante nature of lex cryptographica, which turns it into a prefigurative apparatus that can implement (and enforce) a set of rules agreed on by the community. Practice and theory work simultaneously. Critical Blockchain Art represents a particular type of utopia convened by the community, which is put to work through the technology.

The study of sociologist Anton Törnberg became particularly relevant when I was writing this book and conceptualizing blockchain as a site for place-based politics. My aim was to understand how this technology could offer a symbolic and material space for experimenting with dissenting futures. Törnberg's work is grounded in the convergence of transition studies, socio-technical change, and prefigurative politics—offering a useful framework to think about blockchain not merely as a technical infrastructure, but also as a contested space where imaginaries are constructed and negotiated. His perspective is valuable precisely because it does not assume innovation to be neutral. Instead, it shows how technologies become fields of struggle between competing visions of the future. This is where the study of blockchain cannot be separated from the structures of capitalism. The theoretical tools I draw on often emerge from studies of how markets absorb and reshape innovation, how new technologies are commodified. But they can also be read as tools for understanding how alternative social formations emerge from within these systems. Blockchain is a double-edged sword. It is exploited by markets to deepen speculative finance, yet also reappropriated by artists who use it to imagine and construct countersystems. Both forces are reimagining economic life, but with radically different ambitions: one to extend dominance, the other to fracture it.

In the 1990s, transition studies started investigating the technical equivalence to prefigurative politics. It considered how and when new technical innovations incubated in a niche manage to break out to replace technical solutions already established in society. Within transition studies, a niche is defined as "a space for experimentation shielded from market competition where radical, path-breaking innovations could be developed."[28] Niches therefore act as a protective buffer to secure, nurture, and empower.[29] They also offer protection that avoids the innovation being rejected at an early stage by society. And this understanding was, obviously, very important to see how blockchain could potentially support radical imaginaries.

In this research Törnberg mentions several niches. Free spaces are one type and provide an incubator for innovations that cannot survive within a given political infrastructure and its norms, which are already completely consolidated in society. That is, it provides a home to protect the innovation from hegemonic systems of thought. Therefore, these small-scale niches are pivotal in societal transitions as they provide a proactive space where prefigurative innovation can flourish. Or, as Chandra Mukerji puts it, free spaces provide "shelter for dreams of possibilities that lie outside political discourse."[30] For Törnberg, too, free spaces are especially relevant in radical prefiguration, since they act as cultural laboratories that permit activists to wrestle hegemonic narratives, both cultural and institutional. In them, activists can construct embryonic countercultures that contravene hegemonic cultural paradigms and their implicit common sense.[31] Artists working on socially engaged practices work analogously, creating micro-utopias or pilot projects like Ensembl.

Ensembl is a blockchain project managed by Samson Young, artist, and performer; writer, filmmaker, and anthropologist Massimiliano Mollona; and Andrew Crowe and Ashley Lee Wong from MetaObjects, an art and creative technology studio. This project aims to create a DAO that reflects the collaborative and changing nature of music performances. In doing so, they explore how the author's role is changing and probe emerging modes of artistic collaboration. These types of projects use blockchain as a tool for radical imaginings, thinking of new forms of democratization and governance that could facilitate a more equal art world. They help imagine a pluriverse where change appears across realms and timeframes according to the community that instigates a new formulation of the technology.

These artworks use lex cryptographica as a tool to configure their prefigurative yearning. Therefore, Critical Blockchain Art becomes a type of prefigurative art, which could be defined as experimental practices that convey an alternative system against an external oppression. "It is a matter of performing particular initiatives in order to show that change is possible," asserts art historian Ewa Domanska.[32] Critical Blockchain Art prefigures a coming society at a microlevel and aims to affect change on a macrolevel by prompting radical social change through practice. Ensembl, for instance, constitutes that free space for experimentation.

There are different pathways whereby a free space can successfully define the result of a prefigurative attempt at social change. One of them describes a given change that is somehow compatible with the regime and implemented as an add-on.[33] We can apply this to artworks minted on NFTs, for instance, as the application seems to solve certain problems, but it doesn't challenge the underlying logic. An NFT offers the possibility of tracing provenance and creates a sustainable remuneration to the artist, but it doesn't directly question issues such as scarcity or ownership. After the innovation is incorporated into the infrastructure of the old regime, it triggers changes in its basic architecture; for example, collectors, investors, and museums acquire these digital works en masse. Although these changes aren't radical in themselves, they start new patterns of interactions that lead to new forms of organizing that could potentially undermine the regime, according to Törnberg.[34]

I believe that Critical Blockchain Art represents a later stage on Törnberg's path to social change. These practices create a fluid space for prefiguration that nurtures alternative social paradigms grounded on non-capitalocentric values. Not only does Critical Blockchain Art spread potential alternative technological uses beyond the commodifiable outputs, but it also triggers a collateral conversation that raises awareness about the technology in general and inquiry about the unfolding social uses. For instance, if we go back to *Holly+*, blockchain empowers experimentation with AI in music, while the workings of the DAO makes possible the desire of unleashing creativity without copyright. *Holly+* does so through the offspring of the voice model, which pre-enacts that social imaginary by means of a DAO that stewards the voice model as a commons.

If we consider artist-driven blockchain projects as free spaces, we could imagine the ways in which the technology could support the social innovation we aim for. As a free space, it offers a shielded place for rehearsals, untouched by market or societal dynamics, evolving and creating a multiverse of agonistic counter-hegemonic proposals. Critical Blockchain Art functions exactly in this way: it reveals a free space where one can prefiguratively embody any social alternative.

Moving away from sociology and back to the art world, the act of dislocating time is found in other practices such as theater. Rimini Protokoll is a German postdramatic theater company, and one of its directors, Stefan Kaegi, calls these gestures of time-making "anticipatory simulation games," that is, "re-enactments where viewers, players, users, and concerned persons themselves climb into stranger's skins."[35] However, he continues, the result is often not a reconstruction of the past but rather, a speculative reflection on our present and future that prepares us for the arrival of that future.[36] In this way, reenactment (or better said, a pre-enactment, as I will later explain) helps anticipate an image of our future from our experience of today.

Like many other artists working with blockchains, Black Swan unlocks Web3's world-building capacity through durational participatory performances using LARP. The collective investigates how creative communities can seize the value that is produced by their artistic processes and create a sustainable economic model. Some years ago, I curated a discursive program for the Van Abbemuseum for which I invited the Black Swan collective to develop a session that took the shape of a performative dinner. After the session, Calum Bowden, one of the Black Swan artists, explained the concept of "play as experimentation to try to understand different protocols in different technical systems." According to the artists, this methodology is similar to peer support or pure peer review as it reveals the interdependence between the art worlds. I like to think of LARP sessions as the free spaces described by Törnberg:[37] protected places for experimentation.

Marchart refers specifically to LARP methodologies as forms of pre-enactment, expressing artistic anticipation of a political event. Whether in the shape of prefiguration or pre-enactment, this dislocated time is a productive condition that permits the exploration of future politics, and how they are interlaced with the past by practicing them in the present. Performance historian Shannon Jackson specifies that "to enact again might be to re-contextualise, to take out of context and place in a new one, and thereby to wrestle with a poor context so that it can make a different sense, or a different non-sense, anew."[38] The same goes for other practitioners in the field. The Sphere, for instance, hosts research labs called "Digital Soulsearching," which also use LARPing methodologies to change and collectively reimagine an unsustainable reality for artists in late-stage capitalism.[39] That is how Critical Blockchain Art projects, like the works of Black Swan and the Sphere, generate free spaces that pre-enact their social imaginary. This action allows us, the spectators, to participate and become coauthors of a particular value system, which we perform prefiguratively by LARPing their shared project to autonomy. The temporary fluctuation of a free space enables artists working with blockchains to develop and practice a techno-social apparatus adapted to the value of a community.

Structures of Belonging

Wisdoms for Neknel is a project by the collective Keiken that uses artificial intelligence and blockchain technology to prefigure an alternative universe, called Neknel, in which labor no longer exists and there are only cosmic goals and shared purposes. The artists frame Neknel as a protopia, meaning a society that makes incremental progress over a long period of time rather than solving all its problems (as in a utopia) or falling into dire dysfunction (as in a dystopia). A protopia is a less idealistic version of utopia and more optimistic than a dystopia. It gives hope. In it, consciousness has expanded and is no longer limited to the physical realm to include new forms of wisdom and understanding. $WISDOM, Neknel's currency, represents knowledges instead of extraction-driven markets. It is the source of change and value in Neknel.

To develop the $WISDOM currency, Keiken hosted a series of conversations with experts from diverse fields who have dedicated their lives to the pursuit of wisdom. The objective of these conversations is to unveil the fundamental truths and wisdom that underpin our base reality. Every conversation is synthesized by an AI model called Beletnom, which crafts succinct passages that are contained in $WISDOM Vessel NFTs. Each of the ERC721 NFTs is a generative artwork that reacts to content of the conversation and contains a different amount of $WISDOM. The $WISDOM currency pre-enacts a world that circumvents the logic of capitalism by creating a currency that queers economic languages to convey tokens that perform a language of economic diversity. It makes visible and thus valuable the generation and dissemination of knowledge in a community. This recalls Strathern's understanding of value as relational, and a representation of a specific connection between members of a community. In the same vein, the gesture Strathern described as "giving value" finds in blockchain its representation as kin tokens, where the technology provides a structure of belonging. Here, the NFTs owners become players partaking in this collective act of imagination that helps conjure this alternative social imaginary; they are active agents in the process of "making visible" a relationship and, with it, a particular value system. Acting as a simulacrum, Neknel dislocates time to describe a desired unwritten future that prompts reflection on the future of value. And, by these means, it proposes life otherwise, as if the market were relegated to the margins of economic thought and replaced with a currency made of collective wisdom to care for a new society underway.

A structure of belonging symbolizes a kin architecture where the project constituents are united by a shared social imaginary. Blockchain scaffolds social relations, becoming a social connective in a decentralized community. But, no one joins a community if there is no relationship between the participants. Although one could argue that trustlessness manufactures trust to facilitate large-scale social organizing, we also have to admit that one needs a ton of trust to be part of a community that is reminiscent of a Ponzi scheme. Consider *Holly+*, the DAO that people participate in because they like Holly Herndon's music and share the same values, and likely aspire to construct and be part of the same future configuration. Blockchain technology facilitates a structure of belonging for a decentralized community of supporters of *Holly+*, making it possible to continue their project of AI experimentation. The same happens with +Life constituents who would benefit from the DAO's collective knowledge to tailor their investment portfolio to sustainable assets, but surely they are united by something more expansive: the fact that they place ecological values at the top of their social imaginary.

Barbara Cueto: Art and blockchains are quite a difficult topic both in the art world and in crypto, and usually it gets reduced to a conversation about NFTs. What do you think about them?

Geert Lovink: The NFT hype of early 2021 coincided [with] and I cannot really disassociate [it from] the COVID-19 isolation drama. Will there be a second wave? If so, it will not happen in the form of NFTs. I personally hope that it will address the much wider issue, namely of how artists are going to make a living. And the question of what is a fair price. Through self-organization, a lot can be done. And I think that digital artists will have to come together, [though] I'm not saying they have to unionize. This is a call for experimentation with new forms of togetherness.

Critical blockchain practices are propositions of alternative social configurations and, thus, intrinsically related to collective forms of identification. Like any social practice, as Bishop points out, the technology "engages not only with a specific group of people, but also with their social and cultural concerns. . . . It grapples with social conditions, political context and unique history."[40] In Critical Blockchain Art, this affective connection finds its way in through three complementary tactics: the structure provided by the meshworking systems in digital activism, the common goal of achieving change on a local scale, and the repercussion of prefiguration. And this connection materializes in the idea of kin tokens, a representation of the participation in a community, embodying Strathern's description of relational value. Tokens serve as precisely as proxy for value but, also, denote a relationship between token holders, for example, in Channel, whose tokens gave access to the Discord community, along with access to the podcast and future Web3 tools. And, in Dayra, it became the connecting feature between a community whose members exchange goods and services. In *Autonomous Forest,* tokens are NFTs representing the topology of the forest, and also give decision-making power to the owner and participant in terra0's exercise of shared responsibility. Kin tokens become assets that symbolize belonging to a community that shares goals and belief systems and that supports artistic experimentation.

The sense of political belonging can also be found in prefiguration, as it is a value-loaded activity that provokes an affective union among the participants in a social movement. Both come to be spheres of alternative social production within the participating agents. And, as result, this process creates a common identity and authority for acting politically.[41] Naturally, this kinship is imbued with a particular value system that is put to the fore, as prefiguration is "the continuous exercise of testing the imaginary landscapes against the necessities and subterranean flows of daily life."[42] By participating in a social movement, one shares a value system that describes a social imaginary. Blockchain's worldling ability enacts those imaginaries.

If we look at the structure of a meshwork system, it is based on connecting the constituents of a social movement utilizing digital technologies. Meshworks transpose the concept of open-source cooperation to the physical world, creating a peer-to-peer support network, both online and offline. This informal type of decentralization generates kinship between the peers, which gets amplified that the action of prefiguration. Since distributed ledger technology formalizes those meshwork systems, it also adopts the underlying collective sense of belonging. Hence, the technology in itself becomes the locus of possibility for a decentralized community. Blockchain, as a site for place-based politics, acts as the manifestation of worldviews and knowledges, and with them, creates a collective sense of belonging.

This context connects with socially engaged art, which are projects that focus on participation and engagement with specific communities, with the goal of achieving change on a local scale. These artworks, like many artists working with blockchains, are concerned with the effects of late capitalism, especially the growing sense of individualism that leads to the dismantling of the collective. They focus on the *making of a community*, and the development of a collaboration system. Blockchains constitute radical approaches to governance that create different orders and flows in a society. In *Wisdoms for Neknel* the goal is to radically imagine a world where work no longer exists and value is determined by wisdom. In acquiring their NFT, one becomes part of their protopia.

Infrastructure of Critique

As many have already said, blockchain technology has a radical disruptive potential in terms of economics, politics, and governance.[43] However, blockchain is still a nascent technology, and its effects and potentialities will be determined by its future development and uses. Amid both praise and controversy, Bitcoin is, so far, the best-known example of the technology. It has launched a much-needed conversation about international financial systems, challenging the notion of value at large.

Beyond this financial analysis, blockchain has the potential to radically question the very system that upholds the hegemonic orders that determine our social institutions. Previously I have considered the ways in which blockchain could become a socio-technological structure that can arrange social life following non-capitalocentric values, giving priority to the making of a community and, thus, focusing on fostering social surplus. Digital art, in turn, is a critical practice that problematizes the effects of neoliberalism and is attuned to the necessities and claims of a postdigital society. In Critical

Blockchain Art these two characteristics collide in the notion of the infrastructure of critique, and provokes consideration of the technology both as a system of analysis and as a mechanism of subversion. For example, in *Holly+*, blockchain is used to support a critique of the way music is consumed and distributed, and it also provides an alternative to circumvent copyright laws and, instead, generates a commons. So, the technology, becomes in itself the infrastructure of critique, as it becomes a structure to both criticize and disrupt the system that hosts the project.

On July 15, 2021, artist Hito Steyerl staged an occupation of the Bundeskunsthalle in Bonn, Germany, not through physical presence but through the digital infrastructure of the blockchain. By registering the museum's address on the Ethereum blockchain and asserting ownership via an NFT, Steyerl exposed the precarious foundations of property claims in the rapidly expanding market for digital ownership certificates. This satirical gesture not only critiqued the speculative logic of NFTs, but also engaged with the radical potential of blockchain technology, which envisions a decentralized redistribution of power over financial and cultural assets. The project *Who Controls the Bundeskunsthalle?* also involved two other collectives: the Department of Decentralization, which in the public event showed how blockchain can facilitate greater public and artistic co-design; and the research collective Other Internet, which developed a voting tool designed to enhance transparency in the allocation of money and resources. The outcome was *StrikeDAO*, an experiment in participatory governance for art institutions. During a performative presentation, three models were put up for a vote, and visualized through a vote-based re-edit of Steyerl's eponymous 2010 video piece.[44] This means that the voting process directly informs a dynamic reinterpretation of Hito Steyerl's *Strike*, generated by software that integrates the distribution of votes into a new edit of the work. In this way, Steyerl extends the principles of decentralization to her own artistic practice, while also utilizing blockchain embedding as an infrastructure of critique. *StrikeDAO* questions the gatekeeping and funding allocation of the institutional setting while also enabling a new form of production and dissemination of Steyerl's work.

Projects like *StrikeDAO* utilize distributed ledger technology as a system of analysis of the overarching institutional framework hosting the project, and also provide a subversive tool to renegotiate the pitfalls of hegemonic systems where it sits. *StrikeDAO* proposes an alternative imaginary: an art world where its constituents can voice their preferences by endowing them with voting power. Philosopher Chantal Mouffe emphasizes the potential of art to undermine the social imaginary needed to reproduce capitalism. She explains that "to apprehend their political potential, we should visualise forms of artistic resistance as agonistic interventions within the context of counter-hegemonic struggles."[45] Each artistic project performs a distinct order that comes to introduce a different counter-hegemonic practice. *StrikeDAO*, like any other Critical Blockchain Artwork, *performs* the political. These experiments call into question previously sedimented practices and tentatively propose another form of hegemony. By doing so, they state a difference, and with it, an unresolvable conflict.

This type of disagreement is known as a form of agonism: a struggle between two adversaries fighting for their interpretation to become a hegemony, but without casting doubt on the legitimacy of their opponent's right to fight.[46] Mouffe thinks of agonism as the "tamed version of antagonism," a legitimate way to voice dissent that can prevent democratic disaffection and political extremism.[47] The potential of agonism is, consequently, immanently present in artistic practices that use blockchain, because they always embody an alternative vision of a given hegemony. They put forward an opposite order that lives in parallel to the reality they populate. *StrikeDAO* proposes a collective form of decision-making for art institutions, challenging their gate-keeping. +Life provides a collective way to create a sustainable portfolio, questioning traditional stocks assemblages such as ETFs.

It is through the infrastructure of critique that these artistic practices are able to examine and disrupt a given order. Distributed ledger technology systematically and thoroughly engages with a form of critique that represents noncompliance with the hierarchies of the networks of power. Dayra, for instance, subtly considers the pitfalls of a system of cultural production in Palestine, and also provides an alternative that expands beyond the limits of the art world to create a resilient system of cooperation. The subversive potential rests on the tentative possibility of enacting an alternative and creating a new form of aesthetic dissent that expands the reach and function of institutional critique. It is not just a proposal, it has agency. It provides a governance[48] structure with new alternatives adapted to the necessities of each community, which bestows the capacity to debunk the sedimented practices that convey the hegemonic systems of today. However, the technology is not a singular answer, but a plural and diverse response, which uses the plasticity of its affordances to adapt to the shared values and goals of each community, determining its socio-economical organization. Chantal Mouffe asserts, "Any order is always the expression of a particular configuration of power relations."[49] Therefore, it is not definitive but a provisional and precarious articulation of contingent practices,[50] meaning that any order could also be challenged and subverted by any other counter-hegemonic practice. The instability is also an opportunity, one that enables these artistic practices to rehearse alternative social production and reproduction by radically engaging with the affordances to create new social imaginaries.

Blockchain is a sandbox for institution-making. The flexibility of the affordances can compose any structure to support any given value system, and this is how Critical Blockchain Art composes counter-hegemonic orders. Each and every project uses the instability of the limits between the social and the political, and all posit possible ways of renegotiating and displacing hegemonic systems. Through this infrastructure of critique, these projects embody adversarial proposals and, thus, put forward agonistic pluralism, which endows them with political agency. As a result, Critical Blockchain art can be considered a mix of both politics and aesthetic experiments, which bring forward an aesthetic form of critique. It is both world-building and subversive.

AGONISTIC MULTIVERSES: PRE-ENACTMENT AND THE POLITICAL AGENCY OF CRITICAL BLOCKCHAIN ART

Barbara Cueto: Critical Blockchain Art creates micro-utopias or pilot projects. How much would they need to scale up? Could they become gestures of revolution?

Geert Lovink: We need to think in the direction of Robin Hood. And steal from the rich and give to the poor but on a technological level. We need to think about radical forms of redistribution. Let's steal 5 percent of Elon Musk's wealth and do something useful with it. I would not be against that.

Critical Blockchain Art is in a limbo between art, tech, and science: part direct theory, part R&D experiment, part start-up dreamscape. It is a slippery notion that finds its way in the fluidity of the art world but spreads much further. That is why and how Critical Blockchain Art acts as a communicating vessel: it fosters a reciprocal exchange where technology reshapes artistic practice, and art reconfigures how we understand technology.

The artist-driven blockchain configurations play on the texture of feeling and the embodied knowledges created by the technology. Critical Blockchain Art engages with and puts to work structures of belonging, dislocated time, and infrastructure of critique to bring forth the future in the now. These forms of aesthetic dissent turn into a speculative performance whereby artists and likeminded agents anticipate a society to come, since they can engender a new, digital, and decentralized space of agonistic politics. I believe it is one of the best ways that we now have to understand, to see, to feel what an imagined postcapitalist blockchain could look like.

At the heart of Critical Blockchain Art lies the concept of pre-enactment. These projects do not merely replicate past events or critique the present; instead, they deduce learnings to craft potential futures. By inviting audiences to engage in building societies ahead of their time, these artworks dislocate our experience of temporality, endowing them with a unique political agency. Unlike reenactments that revive historical events, pre-enactments cast a critical, often dystopian view into our future. As political theorist Oliver Marchart explains, "the point of pre-enactment [is] to critically extrapolate from contemporary developments an image of our social or political future."[51] To him, this practice is rendered in live-action role-playing. He clarifies that "rather than reviving events of the historical past (such as historical battles), a critical dystopian view is cast in our future by artistic pre-enactors."[52] For example, the work of Yin Aiwen's *Liquid Dependencies* uses LARP as a methodology to enact a future community sharing a social imaginary based on care values. This participatory performance not only makes it possible to experience how this situation might look, but it also confronts the participants with this radical social order. The difference between our hypercapitalist reality and this imagined reorganizing of society becomes a powerful tool. This experience leads to the development of affective engagement since collective identities are built through the types of social relations encoded via token design, hinging on collective goals and values. For example, I curated one of these LARPing experiences with Yin Aiwen at Van Abbemuseum, and we planned for five hours. At the end of it, we were so immersed in the practice of the exercise that we all asked to extend it, to properly engage with this world that the artist created for us, and we, as co-creators, were able to implement our stories in her imaginary. The immersive temporality created a sense of collectivity. As we know, blockchain encodes that weird temporal matrix in the ex-ante legislative tempo; but Critical Blockchain Art plays with it, generating new worlds that implement social relations and modes of interaction that perform non-capitalocentric values.

The pre-enactment gesture conveys political agency through the framework of agonistic pluralism. As articulated by Chantal Mouffe, agonism differs from antagonism by recognizing the legitimacy of conflicting perspectives and treating adversaries as coexisting participants within a shared political space. Whereas antagonism fosters irreconcilable divisions, agonism sustains multiplicity through contestation. Within this paradigm, blockchain becomes a tool for articulating dissensus, adapting its structure to meet the specific needs of the communities that activate it. Rather than imposing a singular ideological framework, it enables diverse utopian aspirations to coexist, constructing a multiverse of agonistic proposals. How does it do this?

Critical Blockchain Art mobilizes counter-hegemonic possibilities through its dual nature: technological and affective. The technological affordances provide a framework for articulating new social structures, economic models, and political orders.[53] Its decentralized architecture allows for the inscription of collective values into programmable systems, shaping governance and exchange mechanisms that reflect the priorities of the communities that activate them. As Brekke argues, a "diverse economies approach to the political economic sensibilities of 'blockchain' helps to articulate diversities and potentials amongst blockchain projects."[54] In this sense, the technology itself becomes a malleable terrain for political negotiation, one that resists universalizing narratives and instead fosters the coexistence of multiple, divergent hegemonic formations.

Hegemonic constructions are not confined to traditional political institutions; rather, they permeate all spaces where power is constructed and reproduced, expanding the terrain of struggle into the fabric of civil society itself. John Dewey asserts that art "strikes below the barriers that separate human beings from one another [and, in this way, the function of art] has always been to break through the crust of conventionalised and routine consciousness."[55] Artistic practices, embedded with diverse subjectivities, thus hold the capacity to envision and materialize new social relations, opening pathways for alternative hegemonic formations. The disruptive power of Critical Blockchain Art lies not in any singular prescription but rather in its multiplicity. Thanks to the Cambrian explosion of governance possibilities, it spawns a constellation of affective interventions aimed at reshaping dominant structures.

Mouffe similarly underscores the importance of pluralization in countering monolithic power structures, arguing that in a multipolar world economic and political models coexist without a singular, imposed rationality. This context creates conditions that prevent antagonistic confrontations from escalating into irreconcilable conflict.[56] As both a conceptual and technical apparatus, blockchain enables the proliferation of alternative institutions, where governance structures are enacted through DAOs and encoded mechanisms of decision-making. As the decentralized ecosystem expands, artistic interventions leverage blockchain to construct counter-hegemonic imaginaries: conceptual infrastructures that unsettle dominant logics. Critical Blockchain Art thus operates at the intersection of dissent and world-building, inviting participants to enact agonistic pluralism in real-time. By rejecting the notion of a singular utopian vision, these projects cultivate a multiplicity of experimental configurations, functioning as rehearsal spaces for alternative social contracts. This aligns with Mouffe's vision of a world composed of regional poles, where political and economic structures diverge without succumbing to a centralized authority.

Blockchain becomes a medium for sustaining agonistic multiverses: a technological infrastructure that enables multiple realities to coexist in productive tension. This malleability extends to artistic production, where artists critique institutions through the logic of blockchain itself. Gregory Sholette's concept of the Mock-Institution, a structure that mimics established institutions while subverting their function, finds resonance in blockchain-based art projects, which simulate and reconfigure institutional frameworks from within.[57] These works navigate the paradox of institutionality, recognizing that any collective structure, no matter how oppositional, inevitably develops governance mechanisms. The challenge, then, is not to escape institutionality but to reimagine its ethical and political foundations. And that is what Critical Blockchain Art allows us to do.

Barbara Cueto: I am interested in small blockchain communities as micropolitical gestures against hegemonic systems, and those are influenced by the workings of community economies. However, one conversation I often have relates to growth and expansion. But, I wonder, do you think we always need to grow?

Katherine Gibson: The scale up argument is one of those . . . that always comes up. But it's just a particular vision, which means just something getting bigger, rather than influence flowing around in lots of different ways and having impact. I think it's partly a problem of theorization of scale that we [stumble] on. And yet, it's always used as if something getting bigger and bigger is better.

And I think we have to challenge that. A community is connected through particular values or particular ethical practices. And that could be global. But the actual manifestation of these activities, or the format in a material place might be quite different. So I think we need to have a more sophisticated kind of relationship to that question [the issue of everlasting economic growth]. Because now, it's coming out of that vision [that] there has to be revolutionary, cataclysmic change that happens in one moment. Otherwise, it's not going to do anything. We need to challenge that vision.

These artistic practices do not operate within the logic of scale, where success is measured by expansion or dominance. Instead, they generate alternative frameworks for value, engagement, and collectivity. Katherine Gibson criticizes the presumption that growth is an inherent marker of impact, arguing that influence is not necessarily a function of size but of relational entanglement, of the ways in which ideas, practices, and solidarities circulate and mutate across different contexts. Artistic blockchain projects thus propose a different politics of transformation, one that eschews revolutionary rupture in favor of distributed, iterative shifts. By prefiguring alternative institutions, they offer reparative moments of anticipatory societal imagination, staging glimpses of futures untethered from capitalist logics of productivity, efficiency, and extraction. In doing so, these practices assert that another world is not only possible but also already in motion. It creates an agonistic multiverse where counter-hegemonic orders do not seek to dominate, but instead coexist, each of them in a continuous negotiation of values, governance, and social relations.

And here resides the radical potential of Critical Blockchain Art: it creates small-scale realizations of a future to come, providing reparative moments of anticipatory societal imagination. By putting these visions to work, artists perform an agonistic multiverse, revealing a multitude of counter-hegemonic orders. These works offer a glimpse of a future that is not co-opted by economic principles of productivity and efficiency, where democratic principles are shaped according to preferences rather than majorities, and where the emphasis on social surplus transforms the sociopolitical context driving communities.

In this brave new world of Critical Blockchain Art, we find not a single path forward, but a rich tapestry of possibilities. It challenges us to reimagine our social, economic, and political structures, not as monolithic entities, but as a diverse ecosystem of coexisting proposals. As this artistic revolution unfolds, we are invited not only to witness but also to participate in the creation of new worlds, to experience agonistic pluralism in action. These projects function as invitations and collective experiences to envision futures where the boundaries of our current reality are not just pushed, but completely redrawn.

CONCLUSION

"For the master's tools will never dismantle the master's house" was the title that Audre Lorde chose for her participation on a panel in 1984 at New York University's Institute for the Humanities. She posed the following question: "What does it mean when the tools of a racist patriarchy are used to examine the fruits of that same patriarchy?"[58] Lorde exhorted the audience to embrace difference, as it "is the raw and powerful

connection from which our personal power is forged."[59] The difference that often disempowers is also the source that triggers the imagination in search of alternatives to conceive the world otherwise. Systemic change comes with new meanings and relations, as old mechanisms cannot be repurposed without reproducing the same structures of power.

Difference is plural and diverse, and it needs imagination to be able to rehearse the myriad configurations that it could take. The political agency of Critical Blockchain Art is its capacity to embody distinctive counter-hegemonic orders based on nonmarket values and, in this way, to create a multiverse with agonistic proposals. Blockchain is a tool for imagination as well as the structure that turns agonistic proposals into organized forms of dissent whose intention is to call into question precisely those sedimented practices they aim to subvert. By thinking through and with the plasticity of Critical Blockchain Art's affordances, artists can practice surrogated worlds-views and renegotiate the financial, political, and social hegemonic order.

As explained in chapter 2, Critical Blockchain Art becomes an expression of agonistic critical art that deepens the project of institutional critique and expands the medium of social practice. Its critique is attuned to the necessities and characteristics of postdigital society, providing a much more nuanced and profound analysis of the current techno-political complex. It can also overcome the institutional system of valorization and foster an engagement that goes beyond the art world because of its formal experimentation, translocal participation, and cooperation. Like socially engaged art, it aims to affect social change and sustain new forms of collectivity stimulating social surplus. Acting like Mock-Institutions, these artistic projects generate collective forms of identification that encourage an affective engagement with their embedded subjectivity.

Precisely because of that speculative approach, Critical Blockchain Art provides the experience of building a world artists would want in preparation for a time to come. It does so through the constitutive process of dislocating time to make possible an infrastructure of critique and a structure of belonging. These practices are rehearsals of the not-yet that formulate new meanings for social structures and prepare new spaces of autonomy. Critical Blockchain Art offers the possibility of bypassing the logic of scale as much as the logic of time. Its political agency resides in its capacity to envision and put into practice new imaginaries that bring about counter-hegemonic orders organizing a political translocal community of agents.

Like Lorde's claim, these art forms embrace their difference and, consequently, they also introduce an irresolvable conflict, which Mouffe refers to as "The Political." Blockchains are their tool for imagination and their apparatus for dissent. Thus social blockchain practices become aesthetic forms of resistance that share their capacity for prefiguration with social movements before them. As a result, they are capable of pre-enacting agonistic pluralism, which grants them the ability to link the present with an unwritten future, and, in turn, to write a future through the practice of today.

CONCLUSION

White Papers on Dissent is an invitation. I wanted to reconsider blockchains beyond the financial aspects, and look at the possibilities of the artistic practices that imagine a world otherwise. I wanted to focus not on facts, but on possibilities. And this was the result: a weak theory, to borrow a phrase from Eve Sedgwick, about Critical Blockchain Art. I did not try to find universal claims, but instead I sought the deviant, the emerging, the alternative, the diverging, and the dissenting artistic practices and theories to compose a tapestry of voices that quietly scream for dissent.

We are living in what Geert Lovink has called the "stack of crises."[1] Together we are cooped up in a mysterious box of disaffections. There is no way out, and no way in. Far from claiming that blockchain could be the solution to save our world, I believe that it could simply point to the right questions. It can enable us to consider, for example, what other types of governance mechanisms might fit our social goals, what voting systems might better represent collective preferences, and how we might reward values that are usually unaccounted for. In the time it has taken to write this book, the technology has gone through various waves of optimism and frustration. But the essence remains: blockchain makes us question the ethos of the structures we take for granted, and pushes us to think about alternatives. It becomes the device that triggers our imagination to think of *elsewheres* and *otherwises*: new ways of enacting dissent and prefiguratively conveying today's utopias.

Critical Blockchain Art integrates politics, aesthetics, and technology, procuring an aesthetic form of critique. These proposals represent a symbolic order, a concrete imaginary that is enacted through the weird temporal matrix of lex cryptographica. This does not mean that dissent is a single answer, but rather, that these proposals configure a multiverse of agonistic proposals, affirming the legitimacy of all conflicting interpretations and becoming the way to voice opposition. This multipolar world based on the different blockchain configurations pluralizes hegemonic orders and, thus, it queers the economic and political models. Concomitantly, these structures break inherited hierarchies of capitalism and articulate social life differently. These different ways of looking at the world contravene the hegemonic order that leaves everyone today with a feeling of unresolved crisis.

This artistic practice represents new social imaginaries that overcome the problems of neoliberalism, be it in the music industry, the art world, or a speculative world without labor. Critical Blockchain Art is able to perform a kind of world-building that anticipates the society to come, giving us a glimpse of a post-crisis future. It creates the new forms of togetherness that Geert Lovink hoped for against the individualizing forces of neoliberalism. It works as a prototype that holds the potential to configure alternatives, allowing the audience to experience these new social compositions, values, and ways of understanding the world as if they had already overcome today's problems. These artworks become participatory rehearsals of the not-yet.

Over the past few years, we have seen the NFT frenzy deflate and cryptocurrencies devalued. There has been a lot of back and forth about the uses and potential of a technology that is in itself tedious, cumbersome, and sometimes inefficient. However, no one has ever thought about changing the world through an Excel spreadsheet. But blockchain, as Geert Lovink points out, gives us the opportunity to explore the meaning of accounting in the twenty-first century. And what we account for is the cornerstone of this book: to account, to measure, to think through a form of value that is not market-driven, but plural, fluid, and diverse. This is why so many people are exploring the ways in which blockchains are renegotiating new social and economic relationships. The success of blockchains is contingent on the redistribution of wealth, as Lovink suggests. Blockchain is not just a digital artifact, but also a tool for radical imagination. And that is how and why it is able to embody concrete responses to the rampant problems of hypercapitalist digital societies. In Katherine Gibson's interview, she posits that many of today's projects still lack a raison d'être, because for many the way they are made, transacted, and traded is an end in itself. Perhaps we still need a generation to speak blockchain properly, fluently. But even if we only fumble our way through it, I believe these practices are still gestures of emancipation, worthwhile proposals that could build alternatives that capture what might still be possible.

In this way, we begin to overcome the binary tension that characterizes capitalism, and feminist, community, and commons-oriented economies can flourish in a techno-social organization regulated by blockchain. The ethical decision-making process can now be formalized at the level of smart contracts. It can make visible, and thus valuable, the often ambiguous social surplus: the cultural and material infrastructure of a social order.

Lex cryptographica, the regulatory framework of blockchain, can enact those new social imaginaries, allowing us to experience in the present what we aim for in the future.

Smart contracts ensure that any future action will always comply with the rules previously defined. Future and present are interconnected parts of the same equation. Although the shift in normative tempo from ex-ante to ex-post makes it difficult to define exceptions and threatens autonomy and accountability, it also gives us a tool to generate a future that is aligned with a collaboratively defined value system.

This book is an invitation to rethink blockchain as an organizational tool that can build pockets of resistance for collectives with shared ethics to describe a similar version of utopia. Naturally, the technology isn't going to code away all our problems. It is, after all, entangled in the very capitalist structures it seeks to question. That is why we need to think about it politically, before it can redesign socially. The revolution might not be bombastic or all at once. Katherine Gibson suggested a different lens, one that looks for influence that flows around and has an impact, rather than scaling up. She suggests looking at the impact of communities around the world that are united by certain values or ethical practices. Similarly, Geert Lovink called for a rainbow of autonomous social movements. And blockchain can provide the infrastructure to support this many-headed hydra: a pluriverse of agonistic proposals. Meanwhile, Gregory Sholette talked about rethinking revolution as spin rather than rupture. Questioning linear forms of progress could help reassess a nostalgic understanding of the future and claim it as a place of possibility. In this way, blockchain's ability to dislocate time plays a fundamental role in the process of emancipation. Through the technology, we can prefiguratively embody an alternative to the status quo. Blockchain is a site for place-based politics for a translocal community united by their quest for a utopia that is underway.

Artists who critically engage with distributed ledger technology have a much more nuanced analysis than institutional critique, and are capable of engaging in a much deeper level than that of socially engaged practices. These practices not only expand those previous movements, but also provide a new framework shaped by the imprint of digital activism. Conceptual artworks represent the first wave of institutional critique, which engaged with the particularities of the medium from within. Despite the dematerialization impetus, these practices were massively acquired by the same art system that they aimed to circumvent. The second wave had a similar fate: they tried to affect the power structures at large, but the art world over-institutionalized and internalized their critique. "The museum is not only the problem, but also the solution!" famously claimed Simon Sheikh.[2] Socially engaged practices intended to overcome the cycles of extraction of the art world by positioning themselves at the outskirts of the institution. If documenta 15 represents the best example of it, one could also argue about its ineffectiveness and incapacity to provoke change beyond a news media spectacle, which, in turn, only echoed their commentary with a conservative backlash. Gregory Sholette says we are in limbo, as we don't have a metric to evaluate successful projects that spill out of the art world. Again, the issue of vocabularies, or the lack thereof, comes up again.

Critical Blockchain Art may very well face the same issues. Both Gregory Sholette and Geert Lovink point to the connection with tactical media as a predecessor that linked art, technology, and activism. Tactical media's interventionist strategies lacked the long-term thinking that blockchain practices achieve by providing an infrastructure that guarantees the autonomy of each community. The interviews make clear the unclear future of blockchain beyond hyperfinancialization. The technology is a double-edged sword: used by markets to entrench their power, and by artists to reimagine economic life. But, at least for now, blockchain still shows a noncompliance with the ethos of hypercapitalism and continues to look outward, outside the art institution, to effect change on a larger scale. The influence of digital activism endows it with a kinship system and a structure that privileges direct action. Since blockchain formalizes meshworking systems, these artistic practices also adopt the affective connection of the preceding peer-to-peer support networks, along with the implicit solidarity and mutual support of that common-based peer production. As the timeless time gets encoded in the praxis, artists can radically imagine another option that subverts the very system that it upholds. And that is their counter-power: they are not reduced to critical statements, they also propose an alternative. They are gestures of dissent.

Critical Blockchain Art deploys digital critical vernacular to engage with multidisciplinary and translocal actors united by their desire for change and their willingness to experiment. By performing the potential of blockchain, these practices become exercises of anticipation of a potential new and diverse society to come. Perhaps I am naive, but like many others, I want to believe in the power of art to create a moment of in-betweenness, a crack that becomes a starting point for counter-hegemonic orders. Judith Butler argued that a state of becoming is created when power is assumed by the subject and this same acceptance is the device for that subject's becoming.[3] This process of being and becoming is always active. Power is continuously repeated, ritualized in practices that need to be broken. To break and dislocate capitalocentrism's hegemony is, intrinsically, the intention of Gibson-Graham.[4] Likewise, the artistic practices covered here not only make possible an agonistic confrontation by effectively putting forward counter-hegemonic systems, but they also expose the political potential of art in postdigital societies.

I do not ignore the technological hurdles, the challenges of implementation, or the risks that must be navigated. I wanted to examine the hopes, possibilities, and dreams for a technology that still needs to be tested, reshaped, and reimagined by diverse communities with their own visions. Blockchain's entanglement in extractive systems is not easily escaped, but in this very tension lies its most generative potential. Critical Blockchain Art offers not just an alternative, but also a lens: a way of seeing, sensing, and responding. It asks us to unlearn what we think we know about value, community, and governance. It invites us to stay with the trouble, to imagine differently, and to act otherwise. And this book, too, was a provocation: a gesture toward the future, an opening toward utopia.

So the challenge is not only to imagine what comes next, but also to begin building it. What if we trusted the prototypes artists are building as real rehearsals for other social orders? What futures might emerge if we allow ourselves to imagine otherwise?

ACKNOWLEDGMENTS

White Papers on Dissent is a collection of countless moments and conversations that took place over many years and in many different places. I owe thanks to so many people for their generosity that I will inevitably forget some, and for that I will feel forever guilty. If you are one of them, please forgive me.

I cannot begin without expressing my immense gratitude to Emilie Sitzia and Mia Lerm Hayes. Not only have you both devoted countless hours of your precious time to guide me as I moved through theories and projects, but also you have always done it with a smile. Thank you for gently pushing me to places I did not even know I could reach.

My deepest thanks go to Geert Lovink for the many catch-ups between Amsterdam and Berlin, which always left me energized and wanting to continue this project, although many times it seemed never-ending. Thank you for your guidance and trust in many other projects away from the academic setting.

To Katherine Gibson and Gregory Sholette: for years I half-jokingly confessed to having a "scholar crush" on your work. Speaking with you confirmed why. Your insights continue to echo in my thinking. Thank you for your generosity, and encouragement.

To all the artists, scholars, thinkers, and friends with whom I've had the joy of talking, working, drinking coffee and wine, sharing meals, and going on long walks: thank you. This book would not exist without planes and trains with no internet, as well as the confinements and restrictions of the COVID-19 pandemic, during which I wrote and rewrote many of the passages that finally appear here.

I feel so lucky to have both a family and a chosen family who have supported me over the years with the blind faith of those who love me, even while being understandably baffled about why I spend so many hours researching a mysterious technology and believing in bewildering politics that do not seem to exist. You all know who you are, and I love you deeply.

And, of course, to Fabian: thank you for listening to my winding arguments as I learned to navigate the many theories and practices I encountered while writing this book. I could not have done it without you.

NOTES

INTRODUCTION

1. Eve Sedgwick, *Touching Feeling: Affect, Pedagogy, Performativity* (Durham, NC: Duke University Press, 2003).

2. John Allen, *Lost Geographies of Power* (Oxford: Blackwell, 2003).

3. J. K. Gibson-Graham, *The End of Capitalism (As We Knew It)* (Minneapolis: University of Minnesota Press, 1996); J. K. Gibson-Graham, *A Postcapitalist Politics* (Minneapolis: University of Minnesota Press, 2006).

4. Diana Taylor, *The Archive and the Repertoire: Performing Cultural Memory in the Americas* (Durham, NC: Duke University Press, 2003).

CHAPTER 1

1. Statista, "Global Revenue of Apple from 2004 to 2024," accessed November 5, 2024, https://www.statista.com/statistics/265125/total-net-sales-of-apple-since-2004/.

2. Macrotrends, "Amazon Revenue 2010–2025 | AMZN," accessed January 20, 2025, https://www.macrotrends.net/stocks/charts/AMZN/amazon/revenue.

3. Software Testing Help, "15 Globally Most Downloaded Apps of All Time [2022 List]," n.d., https://www.softwaretestinghelp.com/most

-downloaded-apps/; Sam Shead, "Facebook Owns the Four Most Downloaded Apps of the Decade," *BBC News*, December 18, 2019, https://www.bbc.com/news/technology-50838013.

4. Marcella Atzori, "Blockchain Technology and Decentralized Governance: Is the State Still Necessary?," December 1, 2015, https://dx.doi.org/10.2139/ssrn.2709713.

5. Slavoj Žižek, *The Year of Living Dangerously* (London: Verso, 2012), 127.

6. Alexander R. Galloway, *Protocol: How Control Exists after Decentralization* (Cambridge, MA: MIT Press, 2006).

7. The Invisible Committee, *Now* (South Pasadena, CA: Semiotext(e), 2017), 17.

8. Vladimir Lenin, *The State and Revolution* (1917), https://www.marxists.org/ebooks/lenin/state-and-revolution.pdf.

9. Zechariah Chafee, "Government and Mass Communications: A Report from the Commission on Freedom of the Press," *The Annals of the American Academy of Political and Social Science* 258, no. 1 (1948): 160–161.

10. Atzori, "Blockchain Technology and Decentralized Governance?," 14.

11. Primavera De Filippi and Aaron Wright, *Blockchain and the Law: The Rule of Code* (Old Saybrook, CT: Tantor Media, 2018).

12. Kevin Werbach, *The Blockchain and the New Architecture of Trust* (Cambridge, MA: MIT Press, 2018).

13. Atzori, "Blockchain Technology and Decentralized Governance?"

14. Sinclair Davidson, Primavera de Filippi, and Jason Potts, "Blockchains and the Economic Institutions of Capitalism," *Journal of Institutional Economics* 14, no. 4 (2018): 654.

15. Satoshi Nakamoto, "Bitcoin: A Peer-to-Peer Electronic Cash," October 31, 2008, https://bitcoin.org/bitcoin.pdf.

16. Edelman Trust Institute, *2025 Edelman Trust Barometer*, January 2025, https://www.edelman.com/trust/2025/trust-barometer.

17. Werbach, *The Blockchain and the New Architecture of Trust*, 29.

18. Jon Matonis, "Bitcoin Foundation Launches to Drive Bitcoin's Advancement," *Forbes*, September 27, 2012, https://www.forbes.com/sites/jonmatonis/2012/09/27/bitcoin-foundation-launches-to-drive-bitcoins-advancement/.

19. The Byzantine Generals Problem is a computer science problem, described for the first time in the 1980s. It involves a situation where a group of participants have to find one single strategy that satisfies the majority and also circumvents failure. However, the only resource available is the messages provided, which either have faulty information or come from traitors. In addition there is no central authority to help and, potentially, there are also actors that can disrupt (i.e., by forking) the process. Paxos was the first consensus algorithm capable of solving the Byzantine Generals Problem. It provides efficient consensus for private blockchains with trusted nodes, ensuring agreement and fault tolerance, but is less suited for public, open networks with high risk of malicious actors.

20. A "hash" is the cryptographic byproduct of a hash algorithm: whichever miner first obtains the correct Bitcoin hash will win the lottery and get the block reward of 12.5 BTC. The mathematics behind the hash algorithm ensures that there is no way to generate the original data from its generated hash. This means the hash only functions in a linear progression. A simple analogy is that you can't produce a real human thumb from a thumbprint. See Arpit Agarwal, "What Is Hash Rate and Why Is [It] Important for Bitcoin?," May 2, 2022, https://medium.com/@arpit.agarwal108/what-is-hash-rate-and-why-is-important-for-bitcoin-d71802d11c21.

21. There are only twenty-one million coins; the amount was predetermined and embedded in the design of the algorithm.

22. Werbach, *The Blockchain and the New Architecture of Trust*, 57.

23. Elinor Ostrom, *Governing the Commons: The Evolution of Institutions for Collective Action* (Cambridge: Cambridge University Press, 1990).

24. Atzori, "Blockchain Technology and Decentralized Governance?," 7.

25. A Turing-complete virtual machine can run any coin, script, or cryptocurrency project; Melanie Swan, *Blockchain: Blueprint for a New Economy* (Sebastopol, CA: O'Reilly Media, 2015).

26. Shermin Voshmgir, *Token Economy: How Blockchains and Smart Contracts Revolutionize the Economy* (Berlin: Berlin BlockchainHub, 2019).

27. Swan, *Blockchain.*

28. Werbach, *The Blockchain and the New Architecture of Trust,* 110.

29. Usman W. Chohan, "The Decentralized Autonomous Organization and Governance Issues," December 4, 2017, http://dx.doi.org/10.2139/ssrn.3082055; David Johnson et al., "The General Theory of Decentralized Applications, Dapps," *GitHub*, June 9, 2014, https://github.com/DavidJohnstonCEO/DecentralizedApplications.

30. De Filippi and Wright, *Blockchain and the Law.*

31. Swan, *Blockchain.*

32. Werbach, *The Blockchain and the New Architecture of Trust,* 149.

33. Werbach, 149.

34. Atzori, "Blockchain Technology and Decentralized Governance?"; David Rozas et al., "When Ostrom Meets Blockchain: Exploring the Potentials of Blockchain for Commons Governance," July 30, 2018, https://ssrn.com/abstract=3272329.

35. I refer to epistemic crowds as like-minded collectives that pool resources and collaborate to create networks of knowledge. I return to discussion of epistemic crowds when I explain meshwork systems later in the book.

36. David Graeber, *Toward an Anthropological Theory of Value* (Chicago: Prickly Paradigm Press, 2001).

37. On scarcity, see David Ricardo, *On the Principles of Political Economy and Taxation*, (McMaster University Archive for the History of Economic Thought, [1817] 1821), https://EconPapers.repec.org/RePEc:hay:hetboo:ricardo1821; on natural order, see Adam Smith, *The Wealth of Nations: Books 1–3*, ed. Andrew Skinner (London: Penguin Classics, [1776] 1999); on command of possession, see John Stuart Mill, *Principles of Political Economy* (1848), http://www.gutenberg.org/files/30107/30107-pdf.pdf; on wealth accumulation through labor, see Karl Marx, *Capital: A Critique of Political Economy* (London: Penguin Books in association with New Left Review, [1867] 1978).

38. Marx, *Capital.*

39. Marx, *Capital.*

40. Ricardo, *On the Principles of Political Economy and Taxation.*

41. Gibson-Graham, *The End of Capitalism (As We Knew It)*; Gibson-Graham, *A Postcapitalist Politics.*

42. Judith Butler, *Bodies That Matter: On the Discursive Limits of Sex* (London: Routledge, 1993), 2.

43. According to Graeber, for "Althusser, everything turns on the appropriation of some kind of a material surplus. Any mode of production is based on the relation of two classes: one of primary producers, the other, which supports itself at least in part by appropriating some portion the product of the first. What makes MoPs different is how this extraction takes place: This is what makes the relation between master and slave different from that between feudal lord and manorial serf, or that between capitalist employer and proletarian laborer." Graeber, *Toward an Anthropological Theory of Value*, 85.

44. Graeber explains that "Appadurai's 'politics of value' largely comes down to the story of how various elites try to control and limit exchange and consumption, while others (almost always popular forces) try to expand it, and the social struggles that result. 'Regimes of value,' in turn, are the outcome of such struggles: the degree to which these elites have succeeded in channelling the free flow of exchange, or, alternately, to which existing cultural standards limit

the possibilities of what can be exchanged for what." Graeber, *Toward an Anthropological Theory of Value*, 31.

45. Gibson-Graham, *A Postcapitalist Politics*, 54.

46. Gibson-Graham, *A Postcapitalist Politics*.

47. Gibson-Graham, *A Postcapitalist Politics*.

48. Judith Butler, *Excitable Speech: A Politics of the Performative* (New York: Routledge, 1997).

49. Gibson-Graham, *A Postcapitalist Politics*, 77.

50. Marx, *Capital*.

51. Jane Fajans, *They Make Themselves: Work and Play among the Baining of Papua New Guinea* (Chicago: University of Chicago Press, 1997); Graeber, *Toward an Anthropological Theory of Value*.

52. Gerda Roelvink, *Building Dignified Worlds: Geographies of Collective Action* (Minneapolis: University of Minnesota Press, 2016), 226.

53. Gibson-Graham, *The End of Capitalism (As We Knew It)*, xviii.

54. Kelly Dombroski, Stephen Healy, and Katherine McKinnon, "Care-Full Community Economies," in *Feminist Political Ecology and the Economics of Care: In Search of Economic Alternatives*, ed. Christine Bauhardt and Wendy Harcourt (Abingdon: Routledge, 2019), 99.

55. This has become a point of departure of many anthropologists thereafter. Graeber builds on Strathern's insights while addressing gaps in earlier Marxist approaches by incorporating more nuanced understandings of value creation in noncapitalist contexts. Lizette Josephides's critique aligns with feminist Marxism but also acknowledges the limitations of imposing class-based frameworks on noncapitalist societies.

56. Strathern's ideas about making visible alternative modes of personhood and value have been particularly influential in feminist scholarship, offering new ways to approach gender and social relations. She also uses a relational approach in her analysis of gender,

emphasizing that gender categories in Melpa-speaking communities are tied to social relations rather than to fixed biological or proprietary roles. Her work moves beyond simple male/female dichotomies, exploring how gender is constructed through social interactions and kinship relations. For her, gender is a "symbol of relations" and a model of society itself, and it functions more like a verb than a noun, providing "models of boundaries and relationships." See also Ashley Lebner, ed., *Redescribing Relations* (New York: Berghahn Books, 2017), https://doi.org/10.3167/9781785333927.

57. Amadeo do Nascimento, "Anthropological Knowledge in Feminist Perspectives: Approaches and Representation of 'Others,'" *Sociology International Journal* 7, no. 3 (2023): 144–148, https://doi.org/10.15406/sij.2023.07.00336; Jasmine Folz and Rachel Smith, "Work/Labour," in *The Open Encyclopedia of Anthropology*, ed. Riddhi Bhandari (2024), http://doi.org/10.29164/24worklabour.

58. "Economic Hubs," *WABA.network*, 2018, https://waba.network/economic-hubs/.

59. Gibson-Graham, *A Postcapitalist Politics*, 91.

60. Jean-Luc Nancy, *The Inoperative Community* (Minneapolis: University of Minnesota Press, 1991).

61. Gibson-Graham, *A Postcapitalist Politics*, 97.

62. Claire Colebrook, *Philosophy and Post-Structuralist Theory: From Kant to Deleuze* (Edinburgh: Edinburgh University Press, 2005), 11; Pamela Richardson-Ngwenya and Andrea J. Nightingale, "Diverse Ethics for Diverse Economies," in *Feminist Political Ecology and the Economics of Care*, ed. Christine Bauhardt and Wendy Harcourt (London: Routledge, 2018), 131–161.

63. Moira Gatens and Genevieve Lloyd, *Collective Imaginings: Spinoza, Past and Present* (New York: Routledge, 1999).

64. Christine Bauhardt, "Solutions to the Crisis? The Green New Deal, Degrowth, and the Solidarity Economy: Alternatives to the Capitalist Growth Economy from an Ecofeminist Economics Perspective,"

Ecological Economics 102 (2014): 60–68; Wendy Harcourt, "Women and the European Crisis," *The Economic and Labour Relations Review* 25, no. 3 (2014): 455–464.

65. Massimo De Angelis, *The Beginning of History: Value Struggles and Global Capital* (London: Pluto Press, 2007), 151.

66. Michel Callon, "Introduction: The Embeddedness of Economic Markets in Economics," *Sociological Review* 46, no. 1, suppl. (1998): 1–57.

67. Laura Lotti, "Financialization as a Medium: Speculative Notes on Post-Blockchain Art," in *MoneyLab Reader 2: Overcoming the Hype*, ed. Inte Gloerich, Geert Lovink, and Patricia de Vries (Amsterdam: Institute of Network Cultures, 2018), 98.

68. Roelvink, *Building Dignified Worlds*.

69. To do so, I follow the study of Lucas Oliveira et al., "To Token or Not to Token: Tools for Understanding Blockchain Tokens," in *Proceedings of the 39th International Conference on Information Systems (ICIS 2018)*, (Atlanta: Association for Information Systems, 2018).

70. Oliveira et al., "To Token or Not to Token," 9.

71. "How Can Dayra Allow Us to Make Use of Existing Local Resources كيف تسمح لنا دايرا باستخدام مواردنا المحلية?—the Question of Funding," 2022, http://dayra.net/.

72. "How Can Dayra Allow Us to Make Use of Existing Local Resources?"

73. Swan, *Blockchain*.

74. In order to expand on these goals, I will focus primarily on tokens with purpose and governance attributes. The collective work of the researchers Cila, Ferri, de Waal, Gloerich, and Karpinski (2020) is significantly helpful for discerning potentials and pitfalls of blockchain structures in commons-oriented communities. See Nazli Cila et al., "The Blockchain and the Commons: Dilemmas in the Design of Local Platforms," in *Proceedings of the 2020 CHI Conference on Human Factors*

in Computing Systems (New York: Association for Computing Machinery, 2020).

75. Rozas et al., "When Ostrom Meets Blockchain," 8.

76. Davidson, de Filippi, and Potts, "Blockchains and the Economic Institutions of Capitalism," 654.

77. Voshmgir, *Token Economy*, 111.

78. Eric Posner and E. Glen Weyl, *Radical Markets: Uprooting Capitalism and Democracy for a Just Society* (Princeton, NJ: Princeton University Press, 2018).

79. Larisa Blazic (activist and artist) and Shintaro Miyazaki (media theorist), in discussion with the author during the public program White Papers on Dissent at Van Abbemuseum, November 2021.

80. Daphne Dragona (curator), in discussion with the author during the public program White Papers on Dissent at Van Abbemuseum, November 2021.

81. Doreen Massey, *Space, Place and Gender* (Cambridge: Polity Press, 1994); Doreen Massey, *For Space* (London: SAGE Publications, 2005).

82. Massey, *For Space*, 9.

83. Richardson-Ngwenya and Nightingale, "Diverse Ethics for Diverse Economies," 134.

84. Harcourt, "Women and the European Crisis."

85. Chandra Talpade Mohanty and Sarah Miraglia, "Gendering Justice, Building Alternative Futures," *Alternatives* 37, no. 2 (2012): 122–123.

86. Harcourt, "Women and the European Crisis."

87. Vitalik Buterin, "Visions, Part I: The Value of Blockchain Technology," *Ethereum Foundation Blog*, April 13, 2015, https://blog.ethereum.org/2015/04/13/visions-part-1-the-value-of-block-chain- technology/.

88. Darcy W. E. Allen, Chris Berg, and Mikaela Novak, "Blockchain: An Entangled Political Economy Approach," *Journal of Public Finance*

and Public Choice 33, no. 2 (2018): 105–125; Tom W. Bell, *Your Next Government? From the Nation State to Stateless Nations* (Cambridge: Cambridge University Press, 2017); Christian Catalini and Joshua Gans, "Some Simple Economics of the Blockchain," *Rotman School of Management Working Paper* No. 2874598; *MIT Sloan Research Paper* No. 5191–5116 (2019), https://ssrn.com/abstract=2874598; Joshua A. T. Fairfield, "Bitproperty," *Southern California Law Review* 88, no. 4 (2015): 805–874; Georgy Ishmaev, "Blockchain Technology as an Institution of Property," *Metaphilosophy* 48, no. 5 (2017): 666–686; Myung Jun, "Blockchain Government: A Next Form of Infrastructure for the Twenty-First Century," *Journal of Open Innovation: Technology, Market, and Complexity* 4, no. 1 (2018): 7; Malavika Nair and Daniel Sutter, "The Blockchain and Increasing Cooperative Efficacy," *The Independent Review* 22, no. 4 (2018): 529–550; Paolo Tasca and Mihaela Ulieru, "Blockchain as an Institutional Technology Spearheading an Equitable Exchange Economy," 2016, https://papers.ssrn.com/sol3/papers.cfm? abstractid=2872916; Swan, *Blockchain*.

89. Yochai Benkler, "When von Hippel Innovation Met the Networked Environment," in *Revolutionizing Innovation: Users, Communities, and Open Innovation*, ed. Dietmar Harhoff and Karim R. Lakhani (Cambridge, MA: MIT Press, 2016), 196.

90. Ishmaev, "Blockchain Technology as an Institution of Property," 681.

91. Tasca and Ulieru, "Blockchain as an Institutional Technology," 18.

92. Ben Waters, "Decentralizing Technology, Society, and Thought," *Hackernoon*, October 9, 2018, https://hackernoon.com/decentralizing-technology-society-and-thought-c59318a8aef9.

93. Yochai Benkler, "A Speakers Corner under the Sun," in *The Commodification of Information: Political, Social, and Cultural Ramifications*, ed. Niva Elkin-Koren, Neil Netanel, and C. Edwin Baker (London: Kluwer, 2002), 291–317.

94. Benkler, "When von Hippel Innovation Met the Networked Environment."

95. Michel Bauwens and Alekos Pantazis, "The Ecosystem of Commons-Based Peer Production and Its Transformative Dynamics," *Sociological Review* 66, no. 2 (2018): 303.

96. Bauwens and Pantazis, "The Ecosystem of Commons-Based Peer Production and Its Transformative Dynamics," 303.

97. Ostrom, *Governing the Commons.*

98. Primavera De Filippi, "Translating Commons-Based Peer Production Values into Metrics: Towards Commons-Based Cryptocurrencies," in *The Handbook of Digital Currency*, ed. David Lee Kuo Chuen (2015), 472, https://www.triple-c.at/index.php/tripleC/article/view/1009/1264.

99. Paul Chatterton, "Seeking the Urban Common: Furthering the Debate on Spatial Justice," *City* 14, no. 6 (2010): 626.

100. Elham Seyedsayamdost and Pieter Vanderwal, "From Good Governance to Governance for Good: Blockchain for Social Impact," *Journal of International Development* 32, no. 6 (2020): 945.

101. Svein Ølnes, Julien Ubacht, and Marijn Janssen, "Blockchain in Government: Benefits and Implications of Distributed Ledger Technology for Information Sharing," *Government Information Quarterly* 34, no. 3 (2017): 355–364.

102. De Filippi and Wright, *Blockchain and the Law*, 51; Lucas Platero, *¿Es el Análisis Interseccional una Metodología Feminista y Queer? Otras Formas de (Re)conocer: Reflexiones, Herramientas y Aplicaciones desde la Investigación Feminista* (Donostia-San Sebastián: Hegoa, 2014), 79–95.

103. Primavera De Filippi and Xavier Lavayssière, "Blockchain Technology: Toward a Decentralized Governance of Digital Platforms?," in *The Great Awakening: New Modes of Life amidst Capitalist Ruins*, ed. Anna Grear and David Bollier (Santa Barbara: Punctum Books, 2020), 185–222, https://doi.org/10.2307/jj.2353884.9.

104. Oliver Leistert, "On the Questions of Blockchain Activism," in *Media Activism Reader*, ed. Mark Graham (Oxfordshire: Routledge, 2018), 379.

105. McKenzie Wark, *A Hacker Manifesto* (Cambridge, MA: Harvard University Press, 2004).

106. Primavera De Filippi and Samer Hassan, "Blockchain Technology as a Regulatory Technology: From Code Is Law to Law Is Code," *First Monday* 21, no. 12 (2016), https://firstmonday.org/ojs/index.php/fm/article/view/7113/5657.

107. Jaya K. Brekke, "Disassembling the Trust Machine: Three Cuts on the Political Matter of Blockchain," PhD diss., University of Durham, 2019, 28; Adam Greenfield, *Radical Technologies* (New York: Verso, 2017).

108. De Filippi and Wright, *Blockchain and the Law*, 54.

109. Lotti, "Financialization as a Medium," 98.

110. Cila et al., "The Blockchain and the Commons," 7.

111. Jerry Muller, *The Tyranny of Metrics* (Princeton, NJ: Princeton University Press, 2018).

112. De Filippi and Hassan, "Blockchain Technology as a Regulatory Technology."

113. Gary Zhexi Zhang (artist), in discussion with the author during the public program White Papers on Dissent at Van Abbemuseum, November 2021.

114. Broodfonds (literally, "bread fund") is a mutual insurance association in which self-employed people jointly make insurance arrangements to cover the risks of sickness or disability.

115. De Filippi and Wright, *Blockchain and the Law*; Swan, *Blockchain*; Don Tapscott and Alex Tapscott, *Blockchain Revolution: How the Technology Behind Bitcoin and Other Cryptocurrencies Is Changing the World* (New York: Portfolio/Penguin, 2018); Paul Vigna and Michael J. Casey, *The Truth Machine: The Blockchain and the Future of Everything* (London: Harper Collins, 2018).

116. Jacques Rancière, *The Politics of Aesthetics* (London: Continuum, 2006); Brekke, "Disassembling the Trust Machine."

117. Manuel Castells, *Networks of Outrage and Hope* (Cambridge: Polity Press, 2015).

118. Galloway, *Protocol;* N. Katherine Hayles, *My Mother Was a Computer: Digital Subjects and Literary Texts* (Chicago: University of Chicago Press, 2005).

119. Brekke, "Disassembling the Trust Machine."

120. Brekke, 64.

121. Brekke, 31.

122. Brekke, 23; Jenna Burrell, "How the Machine 'Thinks': Understanding Opacity in Machine Learning Algorithms," June 2015, https://dx.doi.org/10.2139/ssrn.2660674.

123. Benjamin Bratton, *The Stack: On Software and Sovereignty* (Cambridge, MA: MIT Press, 2016).

124. Jacques Rancière, *Dissensus: On Politics and Aesthetics*, ed. Steven Corcoran (London: Continuum, 2010), 27–44.

125. Brekke, "Disassembling the Trust Machine," 36.

126. Brekke, 39–42.

127. Castells, *Networks of Outrage and Hope.*

128. Steven Buechler, "New Social Movement Theories," *Sociological Quarterly* 36, no. 3 (1995): 456.

129. Claus Pias, "Collective, Connectives, and 'Nonsense of Participation,'" in *ReClaiming Participation: Technology—Mediation—Collectivity*, ed. Anne Ganzert, Ronald Stock, Miriam Denecke, and Isabell Otto (Bielefeld: transcript Verlag, 2016), 23–38.

130. Alberto Melucci, *Challenging Codes: Collective Action in the Information Age* (Cambridge: Cambridge University Press, 1996), 28.

131. Marius Portmann and Asad Amir Pirzada, "Wireless Mesh Networks for Public Safety and Crisis Management Applications," *IEEE Internet Computing* 12, no. 1 (2008): 18–25.

132. Syed Hasan et al., "Building Dissent Networks: Towards Effective Countermeasures against Large-Scale Communications Blackouts," paper presented at the *3rd USENIX Workshop on Free and Open Communications on the Internet*, Washington, DC, August 13, 2013.

133. De Filippi, "Translating Commons-Based Peer Production Values into Metrics."

134. Mayo Fuster, "The Free Culture and 15M Movements in Spain: Composition, Social Networks and Synergies," *Social Movement Studies* 11, nos. 3–4 (2012): 391.

135. Zeynep Tufekci, "Protest in the Age of Twitter," in *Protest: The Aesthetics of Resistance*, ed. Basil Rogger et al. (Zurich: Lars Müller Publishers, 2018), 210–241.

136. Marilyn Strathern, *After Nature: English Kinship in the Late Twentieth Century* (Cambridge: Cambridge University Press, 1992).

137. Castells, *Networks of Outrage and Hope*; Anne McNevin, *Contesting Citizenship: Irregular Migrants and New Frontiers of the Political* (New York: Columbia University Press, 2011), 15.

138. David Graeber, *Fragments of an Anarchist Anthropology* (Chicago: Prickly Paradigm Press, 2004).

139. Marianne Maeckelbergh, *The Will of the Many: How the Alterglobalization Movement Is Changing the Face of Democracy* (London: Pluto Press, 2009); Marianne Maeckelbergh, "Doing Is Believing: Prefiguration as Strategic Practice in the Alterglobalization Movement," *Social Movement Studies* 10, no. 1 (2011): 1–20.

140. Uri Gordon, "Prefigurative Politics between Ethical Practice and Absent Promise," *Political Studies* 66, no. 2 (2018): 523; Ruth Kinna, "Utopianism and Prefiguration," in *Political Uses of Utopia: New Marxist, Anarchist, and Radical Democratic Perspectives*, ed. S. D. Chrostowska and James Ingram (New York: Columbia University Press, 2017), 198–215.

141. Castells, *Networks of Outrage and Hope*, 251.

142. De Angelis, *The Beginning of History*, 151.

143. Adam Hayes, "The Socio-Technological Lives of Bitcoin," *Theory, Culture & Society* 36, no. 4 (2019): 66.

144. Nancy, *The Inoperative Community*.

145. Amaia Pérez-Orozco, *Subversión Feminista de la Economía: Aportes para un Debate sobre el Conflicto Capital-Vida* (Madrid: Traficantes de Sueños, 2014), 92–94.

CHAPTER 2

1. Ophélie Ranquet et al., "A Holistic View on the Role of Egg Yolk in Old Masters' Oil Paints," *Nature Communications* 14, no. 1 (2023), https://doi.org/10.1038/s41467-023-36859-5.

2. Claire Bishop, "Digital Divide," *Artforum* 51, no. 1 (September 2012): 434–442.

3. Paul Crowther, "Ontology and Aesthetics of Digital Art," *Journal of Aesthetics and Art Criticism* 66, no. 2 (2008): 161–170; Katharina Gsöllpointner, "Digital Synesthesia: A Model for the Aesthetics of Digital Art," in *Digital Synesthesia* (Berlin: De Gruyter, 2016); Katja Kwastek, *Aesthetics of Interaction in Digital Art* (Cambridge, MA: MIT Press, 2013).

4. Simon Sheikh, "Notes on Institutional Critique," in *Art and Contemporary Critical Practice: Reinventing Institutional Critique*, ed. Gerald Raunig and Gene Ray (London: MayFly, 2009), 29–32.

5. Hal Foster, "Subversive Signs," in *Recoding: Art, Spectacle, Cultural Politics* (Seattle: Bay Press, 1986), 99.

6. Olive Marchart, *Conflictual Aesthetics: Artistic Activism and the Public Sphere* (Berlin: Sternberg Press, 2019), 105.

7. Lucy Lippard, *Six Years: The Dematerialization of Art* (New York: Praeger, 1973).

8. It is interesting to note the relation here of institutional critique to the research of Miwon Kwon on "One place after another," as her study also engages, politically, with the conditions of the work's site; in this case, the art institution. Miwon Kwon, *One Place After Another:*

Site-Specific Art and Locational Identity (Cambridge, MA: MIT Press, 2004).

9. Foster, "Subversive Signs."

10. Max Bense, *Aesthetica IV: Programmierung des Schönen: Allgemeine Texttheorie und Textästhetik* (Baden-Baden: Agis, 1960).

11. Barbara Büscher, "Vom Auftauchen des Computers in der Kunst," in *Ästhetik als Programm: Max Bense; Daten und Streuungen*, ed. Barbara Büscher (Berlin: Vice Versa, 2004), 229.

12. Martin Zeilinger, "Digital Art between Algomysticism & Fintech Activism," in *MoneyLab Reader 2: Overcoming the Hype*, ed. Inte Gloerich, Geert Lovink, and Patricia de Vries (Amsterdam: Institute of Network Cultures, 2018), 35.

13. Johanna Drucker, "Interactive, Algorithmic, Networked: Aesthetics of New Media Art," in *At a Distance: Precursors to Art and Activism on the Internet*, ed. Annmarie Chandler and Norie Neumark (Cambridge, MA: MIT Press, 2005), 36.

14. Or, as Christiane Paul put it, they were "embedded between various layers of commercial systems and industrial technology that continuously define standards for the materialities of any kind of hardware components." See Christiane Paul, "New Media Art and Institutional Critique: Networks vs. Institutions," in *Institutional Critique and After: Soccas Symposium*, ed. J. Welshman and I. Graw (Zurich: JRP Ringier, 2006), 2.

15. Alexander Alberro, *Conceptual Art and the Politics of Publicity* (Cambridge, MA: MIT Press, 2003), 2.

16. Focus on this abandonment of the museum as the unique scenario for art display increases when I later address blockchain practices within the legacy of Beuys.

17. Paul, "New Media Art and Institutional Critique," 2.

18. UNESCO, *Many Voices, One World*, MacBride Report 659.3 MAN (Paris: UNESCO, 1980), 141, https://unesdoc.unesco.org/ark:/48223/pf0000040066.

19. Marcelo Expósito, "Inside and Outside of the Institution: Self-Valorisation and Montage in Contemporary Art," in Raunig and Ray, *Art and Contemporary Critical Practice*, 141–152; Olga Goriunova, "Participatory Platforms and the Emergence of Art," in *A Companion to Digital Art*, ed. Christiane Paul (Wiley-Blackwell, 2016), 297–309; Paul, "New Media Art and Institutional Critique."

20. This idea is central in understanding how blockchain artistic practices are responses to the sociopolitical complex as well as forces against it. As we have seen in chapter 1, blockchain configurations respond to the texture in which the technology is implemented, whether a hyperfinancial solution or a commons-oriented economy. And, therefore, due to this plasticity, blockchain could also provide an infrastructure countering hegemonic systems of power.

21. Paul, "New Media Art and Institutional Critique," 7.

22. Barbara Cueto and Bas Hendrikx, *Authenticity? Observations & Artistic Strategies in the Post-Digital Age* (Amsterdam: Valiz, 2017).

23. Paul, "New Media Art and Institutional Critique," 5.

24. Brian Holmes, "Extradisciplinary Investigations: Towards a New Critique of Institutions," in Raunig and Ray, *Art and Contemporary Critical Practice*, 53–62.

25. Jason Gaiger, "Dismantling the Frame: Site-Specific Art and Aesthetic Autonomy," *British Journal of Aesthetics* 49, no. 1 (2009): 43–58.

26. Paula Serafini, *Performance Action: The Politics of Art Activism* (Abingdon, Oxon; New York: Routledge, 2018), 2.

27. Claire Bishop, *Artificial Hells: Participatory Art and the Politics of Spectatorship* (London: Verso, 2012); Maria Lind, *Selected Writing* (Berlin: Sternberg Press, 2010); Sven Lütticken, *Cultural Revolution: Aesthetic Practice after Autonomy* (Berlin: Sternberg Press, 2017); Gregory Sholette, *Delirium and Resistance* (New York: Pluto Books, 2017).

28. Armin Medosch, "Shockwaves in the New World Order of Information and Communication," in Paul, *A Companion to Digital Art*, 356.

29. David Garcia and Geert Lovink, "The ABC of Tactical Media," *Nettime*, May 1997, https://www.nettime.org/Lists-Archives/nettime-l-9705/msg00096.html.

30. Geert Lovink and Ned Rossiter, *Organization after Social Media* (Brooklyn, NY: Minor Compositions, 2018).

31. Lessig is a proponent of reducing legal restrictions on copyright and trademark regulations. He founded Creative Commons licensing systems.

32. Ricardo Dominguez is an artist and a digital activist famous for his the "virtual sit-ins" that attempted to overload and crash websites through denial-of-service (DoS) attacks.

33. Garcia and Lovink, "The ABC of Tactical Media."

34. Balász Bodó, a participant in the panel discussion "Blockchain and Activism" in White Papers on Dissent at Van Abbemuseum, confirms this assertion, stating that the language of utopia was written into the digital commons at the beginning of the 2000s.

35. Medosch, "Shockwaves in the New World Order," 356.

36. Gibson-Graham, *A Postcapitalist Politics*, 84.

37. Johanna Billing, JoMaria Lind, and Lars Nilsson, *Taking the Matter into Common Hands: On Contemporary Art and Collaborative Practices* (London: Black Dog, 2007); Bishop, *Artificial Hells*; Goriunova, "Participatory Platforms and the Emergence of Art"; Blake Stimson and Gregory Sholette, *Collectivism after Modernism: The Art of Social Imagination after 1945* (Minneapolis: University of Minnesota Press, 2007).

38. Bishop, *Artificial Hells*, 10.

39. Gibson-Graham, *A Postcapitalist Politics*, 77.

40. Bishop, *Artificial Hells*, 26.

41. Bishop, 22.

42. Sholette, *Delirium and Resistance*, 153.

43. "The Silent University" Arte Útil, 2022, https://arte-util.org/projects/the-silent-university/.

44. "About | Inland," n.d., https://inland.org/en/about/.

45. Stephen Wright wrote a glossary called *Towards a Lexicon of Usership*. The first entry refers to 1:1 scale, which says: "Art and art-related practices that are oriented toward usership rather than spectatorship are characterized more than anything else by their scale of operations: they operate on the 1:1 scale."

46. The two artists are Jon Rubin and Dawn Weleski.

47. I will continue explaining this relation to activist art in chapter 3, connecting this approach with blockchain art.

48. Benjamin Forster, e-mail to the author, 2018.

49. "Los Angeles Review of Books Digital Editions—The Digital Revolution: Debating the Promise and Perils of the Internet and Algorithmic Lives in the Last Years of the Obama Administration," *Los Angeles Review of Books*, August 26, 2017, https://lareviewofbooks.org/article/los-angeles-review-of-books-digital-editions-the-digital-revolution-debating-the-promise-and-perils-of-the-internet-and-algorithmic-lives-in-the-last-years-of-the-obama-administration/.

50. For more information on the topic, see Nick Riemer, "Academics, the Humanities and the Enclosure of Knowledge: The Worm in the Fruit," *The Australian Universities' Review* 58, no. 2 (2016): 33–41.

51. Anne B. Ryan, "The Transformative Capacity of the Commons and Commoning," *Irish Journal of Sociology* 21, no. 2 (2013): 90.

52. Lucy Lippard, "Trojan-Horses: Activist Art and Power," in *Art after Modernism: Rethinking Representation*, ed. Marcia Tucker and Brian Wallis (New York: David R. Godine, 1984), http://voidnetwork.gr/wp-content/uploads/2016/09/Trojan-Horses-Activist-Art-and-Power-Lucy-Lippard.pdf; Boris Groys, "On Art Activism," *E-Flux Journal* 56 (2014), https://www.e-flux.com/journal/56/60343/on-art-activism/.

53. Benjamin Forster, e-mail to the author, 2018.

54. S. R. Ranganathan, *The Five Laws of Library Science* (Madras: The Madras Library Association; London: Edward Goldston, Ltd., 1931), http://catalog.hathitrust.org/api/volumes/oclc/1293631.html.

55. Christie's, "Beeple's Opus," February 16, 2021, https://www.christies.com/en/stories/monumental-collage-by-beeple-is-first-purely-digital-artwork-nft-to-come-to-auction-0463a2c0f3174b17997fba8a1fe4c865.

56. "Episode V. Toward a New Ecology of Crypto Art: A Hybrid Manifesto," February 26, 2021, https://flash---art.com/2021/02/episode-v-towards-a-new-ecology-of-crypto-art/; Josie Thaddeus-Johns, "Beeple Brings Crypto to Christie's," *New York Times*, February 24, 2021, sec. Arts, https://www.nytimes.com/2021/02/24/arts/design/christies-beeple-nft.html.

57. Sholette, *Delirium and Resistance*, 45.

58. Holmes, "Extradisciplinary Investigations," 58.

59. Genevieve Bell et al., "Designing Culturally Situated Technologies for the Home," in *CHI '03 Extended Abstracts on Human Factors in Computing Systems* (New York: ACM, 2003), 1062–1063.

60. "RadicalxChange," n.d., https://www.radicalxchange.org/.

61. "Beyond Cultures of Ownership: Emerging Strategies for Interdependence," September 2, 2024, https://proud-paprika-325.notion.site/.

62. "Beyond Cultures of Ownership: Emerging Strategies for Interdependence," September 2, 2024, https://proud-paprika-325.notion.site/.

63. "The Sphere Manifesto ~ the Sphere," December 7, 2024, https://www.thesphere.as/the-sphere-manifesto/.

64. Billing, Lind, and Nilsson, *Taking the Matter into Common Hands*; Bishop, *Artificial Hells*; Stimson and Sholette, *Collectivism after Modernism*.

65. David Burliuk et al., *A Slap in the Face of Public Taste* (1917), https://www.marxists.org/subject/art/literature/mayakovsky/1917/slap-in-face-public-taste.htm.

66. Thomas More, *Utopia*, trans. Paul Turner (London and New York: Penguin Books, [1516] 2003).

67. David Ayers and Benedikt Hjartarson, "New People of a New Life: Modernism, the Avant-Garde and the Aesthetics of Utopia," in *Utopia* 4 (Berlin: De Gruyter, 2015), 3–14.

68. Reinhart Koselleck, *The Practice of Conceptual History: Timing History, Spacing Concepts* (Stanford, CA: Stanford University Press, 2002), 165.

69. Ayers and Hjartarson, "New People of a New Life," 3.

70. Grant H. Kester, *The One and the Many: Contemporary Collaborative Art in a Global Context* (Durham, NC: Duke University Press, 2011), 20.

71. Martin Puchner, *Poetry of the Revolution: Marx, Manifestos, and the Avant-Gardes* (Princeton, NJ: Princeton University Press, 2006).

72. Fredric Jameson, *Archaeologies of the Future: The Desire Called Utopia and Other Science Fictions* (London: Verso, 2005), xii.

73. Ayers and Hjartarson, "New People of a New Life," 7.

74. Gregory Sholette, "Mocksituation," *Art & Social Justice Working Group, Vera List Center for Art and Politics*, 2015, accessed January 27, 2021, https://veralistcenter.org/art-and-social-justice/glossary/28/mock-situation/.

75. Paul, "New Media Art and Institutional Critique," 2.

76. Erin Woo and Kevin Roose, "This Social Club Runs on Crypto Tokens and Vibes," *New York Times*, March 2, 2022, sec. Technology, https://www.nytimes.com/2022/03/02/technology/friends-with-benefits-crypto-dao.html.

77. "Home," Breadchain.xyz, 2025, https://breadchain.xyz/.

78. Gavin Grindon, "Surrealism, Dada, and the Refusal of Work: Autonomy, Activism, and Social Participation in the Radical Avant-Garde," *Oxford Art Journal* 34, no. 1 (2011): 79–96.

79. In the symposium she led titled "The Avant-Garde Then & Now" (Stedelijk Museum, May 20, 2021), Ellen Rutten positioned the historical avant-gardes as not just artistic movements but also political projects, each negotiating the relations between art, labor, and society. This resonates with the observation that while the Russian

Constructivists became official engineers of the Soviet Union, aligning themselves with state-driven production, the Dadaists and Surrealists sought to renew art outside the institution, abandoning waged labor to invent new forms of collective existence. Rutten's work on cultural memory and sincerity after communism underscores how these early avant-garde strategies continue to reverberate today. By contrasting Constructivism's integration into the machinery of the state with Dada and Surrealism's embrace of extra-institutional freedom, the symposium reflected on how artists and thinkers now inherit, recycle, or resist these divergent legacies.

80. Grindon, "Surrealism, Dada, and the Refusal of Work."

81. Zora's manifesto reads: "We need new infrastructure, something transparent, ownable, accessible, financially sustainable, where we can share the value we create, something for the community, something that's ours. It's not mine, it's not yours, it's definitely not theirs, it's ours." "ZORA," n.d., https://zora.co/.

82. Metalabel has now abandoned all blockchain-based infrastructure but their "About" text says: "A metalabel is a release club where groups of people who share the same interest drop and support work together. It's a lightweight structure that creates economic, emotional, and creative alignment between collaborators. A metalabel is creativity in multiplayer mode: groups of people pooling skills, audiences, and resources in support of a larger creative vision or purpose." "Metalabel," n.d., https://www.metalabel.com/.

83. "About—Outland," January 16, 2024, https://outland.art/about/.

84. Peter Bürger, *Theory of the Avant-Garde* (Minneapolis: University of Minnesota Press, 1984).

85. Massimiliano Mollona, *Art/Commons: Anthropology beyond Capitalism* (London: Zed Books and Bloomsbury Publishing, 2021), 30.

86. John Roberts, *The Intangibilities of Form: Skill and Deskilling in Art after the Readymade* (London: Verso, 2007).

87. "Channel," 2025, https://www.channel.xyz/profile/0xd561d2869cb33965949733208ab8ad49248ef7e2.

88. Severin Matusek, "A Theory of Value," *Medium*, March 22, 2022, https://medium.com/@severinmatusek/a-theory-of-value-92846a730162.

89. This feature links back to the idea of kin tokens, which facilitate a structure of belonging for community participants, as I will explain in chapter 3.

90. Voiz Academy, accessed 2025, https://www.voiz.academy/.

91. "Neo-Metabolism—09 2025," accessed September 2025, https://n-m.world/.

92. Goertz shared +Life in a presentation we did together at the Festival der Zükunft in Munich in the summer of 2024.

93. Nancy, *The Inoperative Community*.

94. Rozas et al., "When Ostrom Meets Blockchain."

95. Yates McKee, *Strike Art* (London: Verso, 2017), 46.

96. McKee, *Strike Art*, 286.

97. Jordan Beck and Ryan Bishop, *Technocrats of the Imagination: Art, Technology, and the Military-Industrial Avant-Garde* (Durham, NC: Duke University Press, 2020), vii.

98. Joseph Beuys, *Kunst = Kapital: Achberger Vorträge* (Wangen/Allgäu: FIU Verlag, 1992), 45.

99. Caroline Tisdall, "Introduction," in *Joseph Beuys* (New York: Solomon R. Guggenheim Museum, 1979), 7.

100. Patrick Kleinmichel, "The Symbolic Excess of Art Activism," in *The Art of Direct Action: Social Sculpture and Beyond*, ed. Karen Van den Berg et al. (Berlin: Sternberg Press, 2019), 211–238.

101. Chris Jordan, "The Evolution of Social Sculpture in the United States: Joseph Beuys and the Work of Suzanne Lacy and Rick Lowe," *Public Art Dialogue* 3, no. 2 (2013): 147.

102. Joseph Beuys, *What Is Art? Conversation with Joseph Beuys* (Forest Row: Clairview Books, 2004), 9.

103. Joseph Beuys, "Die Gesellschaft als Kunstwerk, 1967," in *Kunst = Kapital*, 167–168.

104. Beuys, *What Is Art?*

105. Joseph Beuys, "I Am Searching for Field Character," in *Art into Society, Society into Art*, ed. and trans. Caroline Tisdall (London: Institute of Contemporary Art, 1974).

106. Dorothee Richter and Michael Birchall, "Editorial," *OnCurating*, no. 25 (2015): 2, https://www.on-curating.org/issue-25-reader/editorial-132.html#.YhP6Wt8o_0o.

107. Jordan, "The Evolution of Social Sculpture in the United States," 146.

108. Jordan, "The Evolution of Social Sculpture in the United States."

109. Bishop, *Artificial Hells*.

110. Van den Berg et al., *The Art of Direct Action*, 34.

111. Richter and Birchall, "Editorial," 2.

112. Erika Biddle, "Re-Animating Joseph Beuys' 'Social Sculpture': Artistic Interventions and the Occupy Movement," *Communication and Critical/Cultural Studies* 11, no. 1 (September 23, 2013): 25–33, https://doi.org/10.1080/14791420.2013.830810.

113. Van den Berg et al., *The Art of Direct Action*, 32.

114. Kleinmichel, "The Symbolic Excess of Art Activism," 236; John Roberts, "Art, Neoliberalism and the Fate of the Commons," in Van den Berg et al., *The Art of Direct Action*, 239–240; Karen Van den Berg, "Socially Engaged Art and the Fall of the Spectator since Joseph Beuys and the Situationists," in Van den Berg et al., *The Art of Direct Action*, 28; Van den Berg, "Socially Engaged Art and the Fall of the Spectator," 28.

115. Biddle, "Re-Animating Joseph Beuys," 26.

116. Expósito, "Inside and Outside of the Institution," 142; Goriunova, "Participatory Platforms and the Emergence of Art," 303; Paul, "New Media Art and Institutional Critique," 6.

117. Paul, "New Media Art and Institutional Critique"; Holmes, "Extradisciplinary Investigations," 59.

118. Holmes, "Extradisciplinary Investigations," 59.

119. Groys, "On Art Activism"; Bishop, *Artificial Hells.*

120. Bishop, *Artificial Hells*; Lind, *Selected Writing*; Lütticken, *Cultural Revolution*; Sholette, *Delirium and Resistance.*

CHAPTER 3

1. Meg McLagan and Yates McKee, *Sensible Politics: The Visual Culture of Nongovernmental Activism* (New York: Zone Books, 2012).

2. McLagan and McKee, *Sensible Politics.*

3. McKee, *Strike Art*, 286.

4. Max Haiven and Alex Khasnabish, *The Radical Imagination: Social Movement Research in the Age of Austerity* (London: Zed Books, 2014), 3.

5. Haiven and Khasnabish, *The Radical Imagination*, 4.

6. Craig Browne and Paul Diehl, "Conceptualising the Political Imaginary: An Introduction to the Special Issue," *Social Epistemology* 33, no. 5 (2019): 393.

7. Cornelius Castoriadis, *World in Fragments: Writings on Politics, Society, Psychoanalysis, and the Imagination*, trans. David Ames Curtis (Stanford, CA: Stanford University Press, 1997).

8. Browne and Diehl, "Conceptualising the Political Imaginary," 396.

9. "Beyond Cultures of Ownership," RadicalxChange, n.d., https://www.radicalxchange.org/updates/announcements/beyond-cultures-of-ownership/.

10. Charles Taylor, *Modern Social Imaginaries* (Durham, NC: Duke University Press, 2004), 23.

11. Zoran Oklopcic, *Beyond the People: Social Imaginary and Constituent Imagination* (Oxford: Oxford University Press, 2018), 13.

12. Joanna Latimer and Beverley Skeggs, "The Politics of Imagination: Keeping Open and Critical," *Sociological Review* 59, no. 3 (2011): 404.

13. Gordon, "Prefigurative Politics between Ethical Practice and Absent Promise," 533.

14. Ruth Levitas, "Ernst Bloch on Abstract and Concrete Utopia," *Utopian Studies* 1, no. 2 (1990): 13–26; Ernst Bloch, *The Principle of Hope*, vol. 3, trans. Neville Plaice, Stephen Plaice, and Paul Knight (Cambridge, MA: MIT Press, [1959] 1995); William Morris, *News from Nowhere* (North Charleston, SC: CreateSpace Independent Publishing Platform, 1890).

15. Levitas, "Ernst Bloch on Abstract and Concrete Utopia," 33.

16. Bloch, *The Principle of Hope*, 144.

17. Martin Heidegger, *Introduction to Metaphysics* (New Haven, CT: Yale University Press, [1953] 2000.

18. Betul Abiral, "Catastrophic Futures, Anxious Presents: Lifestyle Activism and Hope in the Permaculture Movement in Turkey," master's thesis, Sabancı University, 2015, 96.

19. Levitas, "Ernst Bloch on Abstract and Concrete Utopia."

20. Miguel Abensour, "The History of Utopia and the Destiny of Its Critique," in *Political Uses of Utopia: New Marxist, Anarchist, and Radical Democratic Perspectives*, ed. S. D. Chrostowska and James Ingram (New York: Columbia University Press, 2017), 47.

21. Abensour, "The History of Utopia and the Destiny of Its Critique," 47.

22. Abensour, 47.

23. Harcourt, "Women and the European Crisis."

24. Noël Sturgeon, "Theorizing Movements: Direct Action and Direct Theory," in *Cultural Politics and Social Movements*, ed. Marcy Darnovsky, Barbara Epstein, and Richard Flacks (Philadelphia: Temple University Press, 1995), 35–51.

25. Kinna, "Utopianism and Prefiguration," 198, 202.

26. Steven M. Buechler, *Social Movements in Advanced Capitalism* (New York: Oxford University Press, 2000), 207.

27. John Carter and Dave Morland, "Anti-Capitalism: Are We All Anarchists Now?," in *Anti-Capitalist Britain*, ed. John Carter and Dave Morland (Cheltenham: New Clarion Press, 2004), 79.

28. Anton Törnberg, "Prefigurative Politics and Social Change: A Typology Drawing on Transition Studies," *Distinktion: Journal of Social Theory* 22, no. 1 (2021): 87.

29. Adrian Smith and Rob Raven, "What Is Protective Space? Reconsidering Niches in Transitions to Sustainability," *Research Policy* 41, no. 6 (2012): 1025–1036; Rob Raven et al., "Niche Construction and Empowerment through Socio-Political Work: A Meta-Analysis of Six Low-Carbon Technology Cases," *Environmental Innovation and Societal Transitions* 18 (2016): 164–180.

30. Chandra Mukerji, "The Cultural Power of Tacit Knowledge: Inarticulacy and Bourdieu's Habitus," *American Journal of Cultural Sociology* 2, no. 3 (2014): 349.

31. Törnberg, "Prefigurative Politics and Social Change," 89.

32. Ewa Domańska, "Prefigurative Art and Micro-Utopias," *Public History Weekly* 14 (2017), https://public-history-weekly.degruyter.com/5-2017-14/prefigurative-art-micro-utopias/1.

33. Törnberg, "Prefigurative Politics and Social Change," 99.

34. Törnberg, 99.

35. Stefan Kaegi, "Reenactment," *Rimini-Protokoll*, January 1, 2016, https://www.rimini-protokoll.de/website/en/text/reenactment.

36. Kaegi, "Reenactment."

37. Törnberg, "Prefigurative Politics and Social Change."

38. Shannon Jackson, "Performance, Public (Re)Assembly and Civic Reenactment," in *Cultures of Participation: Arts, Digital Media and*

Cultural Institutions, ed. Björn Eriksson, Carsten Stage, and Bjarki Valtysson (New York: Taylor & Francis, 2021), 21.

39. "LABS ~ the Sphere," December 27, 2024, https://www.thesphere.as/labs#anarchive-lab-1.

40. Bishop, *Artificial Hells*, 14.

41. McNevin, *Contesting Citizenship*, 15.

42. Federico Campagna and Emanuele Campiglio, *What We Are Fighting For: A Radical Collective Manifesto* (London: Pluto Press, 2012), 5.

43. De Filippi and Wright, *Blockchain and the Law*; Swan, *Blockchain*; Tapscott and Tapscott, *Blockchain Revolution*; Vigna and Casey, *The Truth Machine*.

44. "Hito Steyerl: Strike—Light Work," July 30, 2021, https://www.lightwork.org/archive/hito-steyerl-strike/.

45. Chantal Mouffe, *On the Political* (East Sussex: Psychology Press, 2005), 8.

46. Chantal Mouffe, *Agonistics: Thinking the World Politically* (London: Verso, 2013) 7.

47. Mouffe, *On the Political*, 20.

48. For example, in chapter 1, I mentioned quadratic voting as a voting mechanism that could help guide an organization such as a DAO in its inner workings by taking decisions referring to the community's preferences instead of only looking at majorities.

49. Mouffe, *Agonistics*, 2.

50. Mouffe, *On the Political*, 18.

51. Marchart, *Conflictual Aesthetics*, 176.

52. Marchart, 176.

53. Hayes, "The Socio-Technological Lives of Bitcoin," 49–72.

54. Brekke, "Disassembling the Trust Machine."

55. John Dewey, *Democracy and Education: An Introduction to the Philosophy of Education* (New York: Macmillan, 1916; repr., 2008), 349.

56. Mouffe, *Agonistics*, 22.

57. Sholette, "Mocksituation."

58. Audre Lorde, *Sister Outsider: Essays and Speeches* (Berkeley, CA: Crossing Press, 1984), 17.

59. Lorde, *Sister Outsider*, 18.

CONCLUSION

1. Geert Lovink, *Stuck on the Platform: Reclaiming the Internet* (Amsterdam: Valiz, 2022).

2. Sheikh, "Notes on Institutional Critique."

3. Butler, *Excitable Speech*, 11.

4. Gibson-Graham, *A Postcapitalist Politics*, 77.

INDEX

Publisher contact:
The MIT Press
Massachusetts Institute of Technology
77 Massachusetts Avenue, Cambridge, MA 02139
mitpress.mit.edu

EU Authorised Representative:
Easy Access System Europe, Mustamäe tee 50,
10621 Tallinn, Estonia
gpsr.requests@easproject.com

Printed by Integrated Books International,
United States of America